THE 7 Points

OF Alcoholics Anonymous

RICHMOND WALKER
Author of Twenty-Four Hours a Day.

Printed and bound in the United States of America
Cover design by Michelle Ogata, WESDESIGN, Seattle, Washington

Library of Congress Cataloging-in-Publication Data
Walker, Richmond.
        The 7 points of Alcoholics Anonymous.
            1. Alcoholics--Rehabilitation. 2. Alcoholics Anonymous. 3.
Alcoholism--psychological aspects.
I. Title II. Title: Seven points of Alcoholics Anonymous.
HV5278.W35 1989   362.29'286   89-16801
ISBN: 0-934125-16-3

Inquiries, orders, and catalog requests should be addressed to:

Glen Abbey Books, Inc.
P.O. Box 19762
Seattle, Washington 98109
Call toll-free (all U.S.) 1-800-782-2239

CONTENTS

QUEST BOOKS
RIVER HOUSE, 46 LEA ROAD
WALTHAM ABBEY
ESSEX EN9 1AJ
LEA VALLEY (0992) 700116

FOREWORD

Richmond Walker, author of *For Drunks Only* and the daily meditation book *Twenty-Four Hours a Day,* wrote this, his last book, in 1956. *The 7 Points of Alcoholics Anonymous* summarizes his years of experience and insight into the philosophy of the 12 Step way of life.

In the introduction, Walker outlines the basic concepts and history of A.A. The chapters that follow deal with the 12 Steps under the headings of: Admission, Fellowship, Surrender, Inventory, Restitution, Live Today and Service.

Walker believed that the A.A. Program was best realized when members share with each other and are involved in A.A. service work. His own life was an example of this belief.

We hope that *The 7 Points of Alcoholics Anonymous* will help those on their journey in recovery, and we are proud to make this important book available again.

Bill Pittman

What A.A. Is

Alcoholics Anonymous is a fellowship of men and women who have banded together in groups all over this country and the world, to solve their common problem of alcoholism and to help others to do so. The only requirement for admission is an honest desire to stop drinking. There are no dues or fees, nor does A.A. accept outside contributions. A.A. pays its own way. Contributions from its members are entirely voluntary. The hat is passed around at meetings for money to pay expenses, but there is no obligation to chip in.

The members of Alcoholics Anonymous preserve the anonymity outside of A.A. and never discuss members' names with non-members. Our names should never appear in print, although this has happened in some instances. At A.A. open meetings, when non-alcoholics are present, only the first names of the members are used.

Alcoholics Anonymous is not an organization. It has no officers or people in authority. It is simply a fellowship of men and women who have a common problem and seek a common solution. Its leaders are volunteers and are responsible to those they serve. All work done in A.A., except for a few paid secretaries at central offices, is purely voluntary. Except for a few office workers, no one ever profits financially from any A.A. work they do.

The A.A. program consists of twelve suggested steps, which the newcomer is encouraged to take in order to achieve a happy and contented sobriety. The program is a spiritual one. We believe in a Power greater than ourselves, which can help us to stay sober. Most of us call this Higher Power God, but each member has their own conception of God. Religion, as such, does not enter into our program.

Each A.A. group is autonomous, managing its own affairs as it sees fit, provided it follows the traditions of A.A. with regard to financial matters, anonymity, and relations with the public.

The Twelve Steps and the Twelve Traditions are printed at the end of this book. We in Alcoholics Anonymous believe that only an alcoholic fully understands another alcoholic. Our program is based on fellowship, faith, and service to others.

Members of A.A. do not accept the premise held by many persons who lack understanding of their problem that it is sinful to drink in an uncontrolled manner. Alcoholics are helped by A.A. to understand that uncontrolled drinking is the most obvious symptom of the illness called alcoholism. Thus the burden of oppressive feelings of guilt is lifted and alcoholics can gather all their strength for the task of arresting the progress of the illness.

Illness can be the result of sin, but it is not of itself sinful. Some alcoholics may have been great sinners, but other alcoholics may have led exemplary lives. With all alcoholics, the course of drinking has resulted in the fastening of the illness of alcoholism on themselves. Most of them have been as little guilty of sin as are persons who are diabetics. Both of these are victims of an illness which can be arrested by the proper treatment, but never cured.

The A.A. program is a method of arresting the illness

of alcoholism. It is available to all drinkers, not only to great drunkards or great sinners. Few of us in A.A. have earned a place in either of the latter categories. A.A. offers hope to the people who have recognized their inability to control their drinking, before the illness has worked complete havoc with their lives, or even after this has occurred. *Here are some common misconceptions about A.A.:*

"Because many misconceptions of our program do exist, I believe that an occasional explanation is in order--to the casual observer, to the visitor, to the new member, and sometimes to the regular members.

First, because of the common outward problem that brings us together and also because of the name of the movement, a frequent misconception on the part of the general public is that A.A. members were all, at one time, hopeless drunks, devoid of character, will, position or morals. If this is your belief, then I suggest that you study further.

Second, many believe that we are a reform movement dedicated to the abolishment of the sale and use of alcoholic beverages. There are many such movements, none with which we are allied, nor do we aim at their goal of prohibiting others their rights.

Another misconception commonly but erroneously arrived at--probably because we ask each member to make an effort to believe in some Power greater than themselves-- is that we make a moral issue of the custom of drinking. We don't. Each member is welcome to a personal belief or religion and is free to follow its teachings. A.A. has not been found to conflict with any religious doctrine, nor does it teach any. It is stated in our literature: 'A.A. is not allied

with any sect, denomination, politics, organization or insti-
tution. It neither endorses nor opposes any causes.'

We are not an organization in the conventional
sense of the word, but a gathering of people in all walks of
life who have decided that we would be happier and that our
lives would be more manageable if alcohol were completely
eliminated from our diet. Experience has taught us, in our
particular cases, that, as a long term plan, an attempt at
moderation does not bring happiness or an intelligent
management of our lives; in fact, it is not possible for us.

We of A.A. do not claim that these desired results
cannot be brought about by other methods. We merely
point to our high percentage of successes and to the thousands of people who have found it easier and more pleasant
our way. Because human beings are gregarious creatures
who seek companionship in this struggle of living, we feel
that the company of others of the same views, hopes, and
objectives will add strength to the individual through the
sharing of experiences, hard-won proven methods, and
understanding encouragement.

The word 'alcoholic' is merely a term made up by
doctors for brevity's sake, and they are not agreed on a clear-
cut definition. For people with an honest desire to stop
drinking, there is no prerequisite for membership in regard
to the kind of alcoholic drinks, the span of time their
drinking has covered, the frequency of drinking bouts, the
quantity imbibed, the quality of the brand of liquor, nor the
degree of dilution.

If your lot on this earth is somewhat less than contented and happy, and you suspect that the elimination of

alcohol might be a start toward contentment and happiness, then we believe that we can aid you in that quest, provided you will make an effort to be honest with yourself."

The beginning of Alcoholics Anonymous is the story of two men, Bill W. of New York and Doctor Bob of Akron, Ohio. Bill W.'s first contact with a way of life which was later to develop into Alcoholics Anonymous was his contact with a member of the Oxford Group. During the winter of 1934, an old friend, also an alcoholic, came to his home in New York, sober. This friend impressed upon Bill the thought that he could remain sober only if he turned to a Higher Power for help, and only if he tried to help someone else to sober up.

Following this conversation, Bill entered a hospital. There he had a "spiritual experience" which was the beginning of his sobriety. After leaving the hospital, Bill began to try to help other alcoholics, but for six months he was unable to dry up one drunk, but he himself remained sober.

Then came a business venture which brought him to Akron, Ohio. The business venture was unsuccessful and in his discouragement Bill was in danger of taking a drink. It was at this low point that he prayed for help, and set out to find another alcoholic. He contacted an Akron minister, who put him in touch with a lady member of the Oxford Group, who in turn put him in touch with Doctor Bob, who was an alcoholic. So it was on Mother's Day, 1935, that Bill W. met Doctor Bob, and this was the start of A.A.

In order to maintain their own sobriety, Doctor Bob and Bill W. set out to find someone to help. At St. Thomas' Hospital in Akron, with Sister Ignatius' help, they found Bill

D., to whom they gave their message. He became the third man in A.A., and never had another drink since that time. The first meetings of A.A. were held in Dr. Bob's kitchen, where his wife Ann served the coffee.

By the summer of 1936, there were five men in the group. Bill W. remained in Akron until October, 1935, when he returned to New York, and continued working night and day to help other alcoholics. Soon a small group was meeting in New York. During 1937, the group broke away from the Oxford Group. This new and independent group, working only for the recovery of alcoholics, was to become the Alcoholics Anonymous movement as we now know it.

In December, 1937, Bill W. arranged an appointment with Mr. W.S. Richardson of New York. The story he told to Mr. Richardson was so sincere and convincing that he called in three of his friends for consultation. A dinner meeting was arranged and Bill again told his story to the three friends, Mr. Albert Scott, Mr. Leroy Chipman, and Mr. Frank B. Amos. Present at this meeting were two other non-alcoholics, Dr. W.D. Silkworth and Dr. L.V. Strong, and six alcoholics from the New York area and Akron, Ohio.

Following this meeting, plans for the continuing of the A.A. movement were very carefully weighed. Emphasis was placed on the desire of the founders to keep this movement entirely apart from any religious organization or cult. Mr. Amos went to Akron and made a survey of the situation there. The result of this survey by Mr. Amos caused him to report that the work being done in Akron was just short of miraculous, and that financial support should be given.

As a result of this, a contribution was received which would keep the work going in Akron until May 1, 1939. This contribution only took care of the minimum needs of the Akron work and it became clear that the situation in New York also required support. Such financial help as had been given thus far had been from the meager funds of other alcoholics. Plans were made during the Spring of 1938 for a campaign among people who it was believed would be interested in the movement.

It was also decided at this time to publish a book which would serve as a textbook for those seeking help for their alcoholic problems. With these plans in mind and with the long-range view of carrying on whatever was wise and necessary to promote the cause, it was decided to form an unincorporated, nonprofit, charitable organization, under the laws of the State of New York. This organization would have general supervision of the work and accept such contributions as might be made. After considerable consultation with alcoholics and interested non-alcoholics, it was decided to form a trust, and on August 11, 1938, the first meeting of the Alcoholic Foundation was held.

Since then, the Alcoholic Foundation, consisting of fifteen trustees, eight non-alcoholics and seven members of A.A., has served as custodian of A.A. tradition and funds. It has acted as agent for the society in matters of national and international scope. More recently, its name has been changed to The General Service Board of A.A.

Acting as advisory body to the General Service

Board is the General Service Conference, comprising seventy-five delegates representing A.A. areas in the U.S. and Canada. This body serves as a link between A.A. groups and the General Service Board. Funds contributed by the groups to the General Service Board are used by the Board exclusively for services related to the groups.

Alcoholics Anonymous World Services, Inc. (formerly Works Publishing Co.and A.A. Publishing Co.) is the sole publishing agency for the society. It publishes the books: Alcoholics Anonymous, The Twelve Steps and the Twelve Traditions, and other conference-approved literature.

At General Service Headquarters, P.O. Box 459, Grand Central Station, New York, N.Y. 10017, a staff handles inquiries from individuals and groups, distributes literature, acts in a public relations capacity and maintains all necessary records.

The *A.A. Grapevine* is the international monthly journal of A.A., devoted to those seeking further knowledge on the problem of alcoholism. The idea of the *A.A. Grapevine* was born in the Spring of 1944. It has become the national monthly magazine of Alcoholics Anonymous. Originally conceived as no more than a local publication for the A.A. groups in the New York Metropolitan area, the founders of the publication were more surprised than anyone to see their creation grow steadily from the first issue, pick up subscribers throughout the country and finally go regularly to many parts of the world.

The initial issue came out in June, 1944, after much worry and sweat, many meetings and long hours for all the staff. At first, all of the labor of getting out the magazine was done voluntarily by the staff, after the daily close of their regular jobs.

The *A.A. Grapevine* never missed an issue and still hasn't. When it began to appear from the steadily growing circulation that A.A.s wanted a publication of this kind and that it was filling and performing a useful service, Bill W. decided the status of the *A.A. Grapevine* should be submitted to the groups. On October 3, 1945, a letter was sent out from General Service Headquarters, asking whether the groups wanted the *A.A. Grapevine* continued and whether they wanted to designate it as the official periodical of A.A. The answers were favorable. Following this, the *A.A. Grapevine* was incorporated and officers and members of the staff were named. The guiding purpose of the *A.A. Grapevine* has been to publish material adjudged to be consistent with A.A. and helpful to sobriety. The editors seek to make each issue a kind of international monthly meeting in print, and a place for the exchange of thoughts by members throughout the world. The several quotations from the *A.A. Grapevine* and General Service are used in this book by permission.

The National Committee For Education On Alcoholism was founded in October, 1944, by Marty Mann, one of the first women members of A.A. It was the beginning of a new public health movement, and organized entirely separately from Alcoholics Anonymous, although the founder was a member of A.A. It was the first step in getting the alcoholics out of jail and into the hospital.

The founder's thesis was that the alcoholic is a sick

person, that they can be helped, and that they are worth helping. The medical man, the psychiatrist, the social worker, and the lay therapist were asked to pool their skills with A.A. in modifying the ravages of an illness to which society had been indifferent almost till then.

The purpose of the committee, now called the National Council on Alcoholism, was educational work on a large scale. Alcoholics Anonymous had proved over the previous ten years that the alcoholic could be helped, and that the illness of alcoholism could be arrested. Therefore, the problem of alcoholism was a responsibility of the healing profession, as well as of the established health authorities and the public generally.

With the stigma of alcoholism removed by acknowledging that it was a sickness, the whole subject could be brought out into the open and discussed. This was an historic event. To get scientific backing, Marty Mann went to Dr. Jellineck, the director of the Section on Alcohol Studies at Yale University. Here the Yale Plan Clinics for alcoholics had been started.

Marty Mann lectured all around the country, forming local committees in larger cities, local information centers on alcoholism, and founding clinics for the help of alcoholics. This organization is having a tremendous influence on public thinking in regard to the illness of alcoholism.

During its years in the public eye, Alcoholics Anonymous has received hundreds of thousands of words of newspaper and magazine publicity. These channels have been augmented by radio commentators and radio broadcasts. Hardly a word of criticism or ridicule has even been uttered about us. While our publicity has sometimes lacked a certain dignity, we can scarcely complain of that. After all, drinking is not such a dignified business. We surely have reason for great gratitude that multitudes of writers, editors, clergymen, doctors -- friends of every description -- have continued so sympathetically and so enthusiastically to urge our cause.

As a direct result of their efforts, thousands of alcoholics have come to A.A. It is a good record. Providentially good, when one considers how many mistakes we might have made, how deeply, had other policies been followed, might we be now involved. In the 'wet-dry' controversy, for example. Conceivably, we might even have fallen out with our good friends, religion and medicine, but none of these things have happened. We have been unbelievably fortunate, thank God.

While this makes fine success story reading, it is not to our way of thinking any reason for self-congratulation. A.A.s who know the record are unanimous in their feeling that an Intelligence greater than ours has surely been at work, else we could never have avoided so many pitfalls, and could never have been so happily related to our millions of friends in the outside world.

As A.A. grows, taking in new subscribers to its program every day, its reservoir of practical knowledge is made available to increasing thousands. Each member, through their twelfth-step work, their talks at meetings, and by their example, helps to pass along to others what they have already learned from their association with A.A.

That is the familiar functioning of A.A., indicative of A.A.'s opportunity to pass on to others the knowledge that it has acquired through personal experience. The opportunity is obviously expanding, as the membership increases. But the opportunity also is being enlarged in still another way. Not only are more people seeking the knowledge that A.A. has acquired, but A.A. is continually acquiring more knowledge to pass along. A.A. has not yet taken full advantage of its opportunity in this direction.

Although its reservoir of practical knowledge is considerably larger now than it was in the early days, little of it has been distilled and bottled for convenient dispensation. We have the familiar packages of the 'coin-in-the-slot' device of calling a fellow member of A.A. before taking a drink, the twenty-four hour plan of living one day at a time, the slogan of 'first things first' or keeping in mind that nothing comes ahead of our sobriety, and several others, all wrapped and ready for the asking.

These are doses of the knowledge that A.A. learned in its earliest days. We have not yet made any real effort to identify, classify, and package the new knowledge that A.A. has been acquiring in more recent years. A.A. grows in pace with the growth of its members individually and their development of character, personality interests and maturity inevitably broadens A.A.

The process is the same for the movement, to a degree, as it is for the individual. When the individuals first come into A.A., they are concerned primarily with staying sober. Avoiding a drink must be their first concern, and during this period they use the various devices which A.A.

has developed. Later on, however, after the individuals have been members for some months, the first emergency has passed. They do not have to struggle as desperately to stay away from a drink. They have built up new habits, associations, and a new pattern of thinking.

If they have been progressing, they have begun to penetrate beneath the surface of their own makeup, and they have also developed a desire to progress still further. These individuals have moved into a still broader area of recovery. They can both contribute to and benefit from the new knowledge to be gained here. So can another, less happy example, the member who experiences a slip after they have been in A.A. for several years, and who have apparently assimilated its teachings thoroughly. What caused this slip? Was the A.A. knowledge at hand insufficient to help them beyond a certain period? Can additional knowledge be made available, which will extend A.A. help out into broader fields that many of its members have now reached? How to extend A.A.'s practical assistance is both a question and a challenge.

1. ADMISSION

First Things First

Are you an alcoholic? You be the doctor. Diagnose your own case. You may be an alcoholic if you drink to build up self-confidence, or to "get up nerve," or if you drink alone, or if you can't stop drinking after you take the first drink, or if you have an unquenchable thirst for alcoholic drinks, or if you will go to any lengths to get a drink when you are "on a binge," or if you crave "a hair from the dog that bit you" and drink the next morning after a spree, or if you drink to escape from worry and troubles, or if you get into serious financial difficulties from drinking, or if you drink when you are "blue" or depressed, or if you drink when you are "on top of the world" or overstimulated, or if you sneak drinks between servings of drinks to other guests, or if the host doesn't pour the drinks fast enough, or if you need a supply of liquor on hand at all times, or if you hide bottles around the house, or if you use liquor as a crutch to help you to face life. *Here are some questions you can ask yourself:*

1. Do you require a drink the next morning?
2. Do you prefer to drink alone?
3. Do you lose time from work due to drinking?
4. Is your drinking harming your family?
5. Do you require a drink at a definite time daily?
6. Do you get the inner shakes unless you continue drinking?
7. Has drinking made you irritable?
8. Does drinking make you careless of your family's welfare?

9. Have you thought less of your wife (or husband) since drinking?
10. Has drinking changed your personality?
11. Does drinking cause you bodily complaint?
12. Does drinking make you restless?
13. Does drinking cause you to have difficulty in sleeping?
14. Has drinking made you more impulsive?
15. Have you less self-control since drinking?
16. Has your ambition decreased since drinking?
17. Has your initiative decreased since drinking?
18. Do you lack perseverance in pursuing a goal since drinking?
19. Do you drink to obtain social ease?
20. Do you drink for self-encouragement?
21. Do you drink to relieve marked feelings of inadequacy?
22. Has your sexual potency suffered since drinking?
23. Do you show marked dislikes and resentments since drinking?
24. Has your jealousy increased since drinking?
25. Do you show marked moodiness as the result of drinking?
26. Has your efficiency decreased since drinking?
27. Has drinking made you more sensitive?
28. Are you harder to get along with since drinking?
29. Do you seek an inferior environment since drinking?
30. Is drinking endangering your health?
31. Is drinking affecting your peace of mind?
32. Is drinking making your home life unhappy?
33. Is drinking jeopardizing your job or your business?

34. Is drinking clouding your reputation?
35. Is drinking disturbing the harmony of your life?

These test questions are used as a guide by Johns Hopkins Hospital in deciding whether or not a patient is an alcoholic.

Alcoholism is an illness of the mind and body. It is an obsession of the mind and an allergy of the body. After the first drink, the alcoholic's will power is of no use, they keep on drinking until they reach drunkenness. They often do not want to continue drinking, they often do not do it deliberately, but after the first drink a compulsion to drink is started and the alcoholic cannot stop until they have drunk themselves into oblivion. A person suffers from alcoholism when they drink alcoholic beverages excessively, habitually or periodically, and lose control over their drinking after the first drink. *Here is the story of a spree drinker:*

"I was pacing the hospital floor. The brand-new psychiatrist was sitting on the bed. 'Well, what made you drunk this time?' said he. So, it started on the day we were moving to the country. My wife didn't want to give me very much to do. She knew that I had a resentment against moving days. All I had to do was to fetch Sandy Hook, our alley cat, from the veterinary where he had been hospitalized for an operation. He had a fighting fixation, induced by a sex-superiority complex. I also resent cats. Sandy Hook was the name chosen by the children, because the cat was the color of sand and had a hook in his tail.

It was a very hot day, but I was cold sober. I got the cat in the car and partly closed the windows, so that he couldn't jump out. But the cat meowed. I couldn't stand it.

I parked the car and went in for a few touches of Scotch. When I got back, all was quiet. After driving about ten miles, I thought I would have another touch or two. In this place where I was now drinking, the proprietor asked me if I was alone. I told him that I was not, that I had Sandy Hook with me. He wanted to know who Sandy Hook was, and I -- by then a little hallucinated with grandeur -- told him it was our Siamese cat.

A bejeweled and elderly lady sitting on the next stool volunteered the information that she was a connoisseur of Siamese cats. She said she would simply love to see mine. Well, it was dark outside and I figured she couldn't see much anyhow because of her age and her slightly crocked condition. So the boss and she and I went out to the car. Sandy Hook was gone. The boss suggested that I had had enough and that I go home. On returning to the bar for meditation and Scotch to sooth my anguish, I decided I couldn't go home. My sweet wife had given me only this one thing to do and what was more she liked the cat better than me. I announced that I would drive back the ten miles and withdrew. When I reached the first spot, I got out and started walking up and down the street, calling: 'Here, Sandy Hook. Here, Sandy Hook.' A large cop appeared and asked me gently what I was doing. After explaining the whole matter, I asked him if he had ever lost a dog or a cat. He said yes and that it was a sad case. In fact, he said he would help me. So he went along the road with me calling, 'Here, Sandy Hook,' and clapping his hands. Cars stopped and their passengers watched the proceedings. Some even waved their handkerchiefs. Finally, we gave up. I invited the cop in for a drink. At the foot of the bar sat Sandy Hook. This happy reunion called for a celebration. Everyone present seemed pleased to join in, toasting the prodigal cat.

Four hours later, I was about to pass the place where I had failed to produce Sandy Hook. I thought it might be unwise to stop because I figured I had had enough. On the other hand, both the boss and the elderly lady might be thinking that I was drunk or slightly nuts. So I decided to show them Sandy Hook. My entry with the Hook in my arms caused an ovation. The elderly lady with the jewels was plastered. She said it was the finest specimen of Siamese cat she had ever seen. So we had another celebration in which everyone seemed pleased to join. When the sun came up over the Bay, I arrived home. I had done the one thing my wife had asked me to do and I reasoned I had done it rather well, considering. I put Sandy Hook on my wife's bed and started to tell her about meeting such a nice policeman. She wasn't interested. So I drank for a few days.

The psychiatrist said: 'You were faced with responsibility, you were frustrated; it's another case of escape.' I said: 'Sure, the cat escaped but I got him back.' He said, 'I'll have to psychoanalyze you.' 'How much will that cost?' said I. 'About 2,000 dollars,' said he. 'No,' said I, 'but I'll give you an acre of land I own on Long Island.' 'Does anyone think that an acre there is worth 1,000 dollars?' said he. 'No,' said I, 'only me.' 'Well,' he said, 'you'll have to stop drinking, and there's only one thing that might help you. And that's Alcoholics Anonymous.' So now I am a member of A.A. and it was, and is, the only thing for me. Because I have faith in A.A. and the people in it and the principles behind it."

The First Step in the program of Alcoholics Anonymous is: "We admitted we were powerless over alcohol -- that our lives had become unmanageable." We must admit that we are alcoholics, we must swallow our pride and admit that we cannot drink like normal drinkers. We must face the fact that we will never be able to drink normally again; that we can never recapture the good times of the past. They are gone forever.

Once we have passed our "tolerance point," we have become intolerant to alcohol and we cannot tolerate it at all mentally. We may tolerate it for a while physically, but after each drinking spree it is harder to come back, to get over the shakes and jitters. Alcoholism is a progressive illness and an alcoholic always becomes worse, never better. Each binge is worse than the last one. Once an alcoholic, always an alcoholic. There is no going back. And there are only three ends for the drinking alcoholic, jail, the insane asylum, or death. *Here is the story of an alcoholic soldier:*

"Really, Private C., I don't know what to do about you!" said the commanding officer, with a perplexed expression. "We had you confined for thirty days and the day after you get out, you disappear, get drunk, and turn up five hundred miles from here. I'm stumped and I'll admit it." The C.O. looked into Private C's youthful face and sincere blue eyes, which were as troubled as his superior's. "Suppose you were in my place. You had a man with your record brought before you. What would you do?" "I don't know, sir." "Do you know why you drink so much?" "No, sir." "Have you ever tried to do anything about it?" "Yes, sir." "What?" "Tried not to drink, sir." "Tell me about it." "I don't know what to tell, sir. I've tried not to drink, but I don't seem to be able to stop. That's all there is to it, sir." "How about overseas? Do you want to go overseas?" "Yes, sir, I do."

In a few weeks Private C. was in Africa. The pattern didn't change. He'd be assigned to an outfit, get drunk, be locked up for a while and then sent back to a replacement pool. In a short time, the whole procedure would be repeated. There were only slight variations. One stretch of three months for selling mattress covers to buy booze and a couple of attacks of D.T.s when he was tossed into the "nut" ward. Finally, the army gave up all idea of making Private C. into a good combat soldier. An army board went over Private C.'s case and decided to give him a "blue discharge," a discharge from the service without honor for excessive drunkenness and he was ordered back to the States.

In a matter of a few weeks, Private C. emerged from the redistribution center at Fort Dix with his "blue discharge" in one pocket and a hundred and ninety dollars in the other. Civilian C. got very drunk immediately. In a matter of hours or days, it didn't matter which, he arrived at his brother's home, where his wife and small daughter had been living. For a while, his brother tolerated the drinking, until C.'s condition became so bad that he was asked to leave. C. then sobered sufficiently to get his old pre-war job back. The first week he worked four days, the second week two days and the third, his last, one full day. C. decided there was no use trying. He might just as well stay in a barroom. His money gave out, but for over a month he managed to sponge enough drinks to stay drunk the entire time. Eventually, the friendly bartender made arrangements to send C. to Bellevue Hospital. Someone intervened and took him home.

After a few days, C. pulled himself together and went to the Veterans Bureau in New York, where he shakily informed his interviewer that he must get work. Seeing his condition, the interviewer suggested that he was not in shape to take a job even if he found one, and that he might get some help at the A.A. Clubhouse at 405 West 41st St. C. was so desperate that he would have gone to the zoo and talked to the lions if anyone had suggested they could help him. At the clubhouse, he talked to various A.A.s. That was some time ago. C. has been employed ever since and "dry."

He says that he feels he's got the A.A. program pretty well fixed in his mind, but he's got to work to keep it there and he never fails to drop in at the clubhouse every day. He finds out something new about A.A., almost every time he does. C. is beginning to see the picture of a whole new life ahead of him and he wants to help other guys who are as mixed up as he was."

Women are also the victims of the illness of alcoholism. With the new freedom accorded to women, putting them on an equal standing with men, alcoholism among women seems to be on the increase. *Here is the story of an alcoholic housewife:*

"For several months my drinking habits were becoming steadily worse. I would not give up hope that at some future date I would be able to control my drinking. Somewhere in the back of my mind I had the idea that I would trot out this 'will-power' others seemed to have and put it to work when I needed it. Somehow, I had been able to shake it out after a night and day of drinking, but this time I didn't seem to be able to face the kitchen stove until I had a drink. Fortunately, there was a little left in the bottle, so while my husband was in the bathroom shaving, I took a 'quickie.' This steadied me enough to enable me to cook our breakfast, mine consisting of black coffee.

As we all know who have travelled this road, along about 10 o'clock the shakes returned. I saw no point in suffering. Another 'quickie.' Needless to say, I ran out of whiskey, dressed and went to the liquor store and returned with a fifth. It now becomes necessary to take the drinks more often. By nightfall, instead of having a clean house and hot supper when my husband returned from work, I was a drunken object piled in bed. I had hidden the bottle in the bathroom and all during the night I would slip in and take a drink. Of course, morning found me a shaking mass of nerves. My husband again left for work with a warning that I must stay sober and straighten up. I didn't know how to straighten up except by taking a few drinks to quiet my screaming nerves.

Naturally, the second day duplicated the first. Also the third and fourth, until at last it would only mean death if I didn't get off the stuff. Finally, I shook it out with the help of my sister. This was the first time I had ever been on such a spree. I resolved never to do it again. But I did. Again and again. Each time it became increasingly worse. My hang-overs were almost unbearable. There was no happiness when I was drinking. It was simply oblivion. I knew nothing of what transpired for days and then remorse would catch me in its clutches.

At last, the voice of my sister penetrated my be-fogged alcoholic mind. She read me an article in our local paper, something about a society called Alcoholics Anonymous. She asked me why I didn't write them. I paid very little attention to her, but after she left I hunted feverishly through the paper for the article, in order to read it myself. I never found it, so I thought I must be 'nuts.' I decided now was the time to use this 'will-power' of mine and at the next party we attended, I trotted it out.

I took only two drinks the first hour but, goodness knows, that 'will-power' of mine let me down. After the first two drinks, I wound up as usual -- drunk again. This spree ended in a sanitarium. There I heard more about A.A. Thinking I would contact them, I went home.

The humiliation of having to be locked up in a sanitarium to get sober kept me from drinking too much for a month, but Brother Alky caught me again in his trap. It was then that I began to believe that I was hopeless. At last, I turned around and faced the woman from whom I was trying to get away -- myself. I listened to her say: 'You are a doomed woman; you know you can't stop drinking by yourself. You've tried many times but always failed. Your future is black as sin. You will either kill yourself or die in a drunken condition. Your husband is sick of you. Even you are sick of the thing you have become. You must have help.' I tried to pray, but no words came. I felt I had wandered too far from God for Him to hear me now. Being unable to hold a pen in my shaking hand, I asked my niece to write a letter to A.A. for me. This she did.

Two nights later, while lying on a couch holding a book before me, wishing I could get some sense out of what I read, someone knocked on my door. I know now that knock opened the door to a new world of opportunity. Three women and a man entered, all nice looking people, people who looked like neighbors but were different, for they were members of A.A. They were alcoholics and they had come in answer to my feeble cry for help.

As I sat there, holding my hands to keep them from shaking, listening to them talk, I thought: 'They can't possibly know what I've gone through. These people all look happy and healthy. They've never been drunks.' They soon dispelled this doubt from my mind. They opened up with both barrels and let me have their stories straight from the shoulder. They asked me if I thought I was an alcoholic, if I was unable to control my drinking. I reluctantly admitted I was an alcoholic, but was wholehearted in saying I could not control my drinks. They didn't tell me how to stay sober but they did leave me with literature and an invitation to attend one of their meetings. I very eagerly seized the literature and as I read each story in the booklet I said: 'Yes, that's me. That's me.' Thus began my new life of sobriety, grateful for any crumbs of wisdom that came my way, thankful to be able to attend the meetings."

Alcoholism is no respecter of persons. It strikes anywhere, among the high and the low, the educated and the uneducated, among all classes, colors and creeds. The old idea that an alcoholic was a "drunken bum" has had to be discarded. The old idea of hiding the fact that a member of a prominent family is an alcoholic -- "keeping the skeleton in the closet" -- has become out of date. It is no disgrace to be an alcoholic, any more than to be a diabetic. The only disgrace is not to do something about it if you are an alcoholic. Alcoholism is an illness like any other illness and must be treated as such, whether the victim is in a penthouse or a flophouse.

I have heard the term 'Park Avenue drunk' used more than once in A.A. meetings and also in conversation around the clubhouse. I suppose it means the man or woman in A.A. who was born into what is known as 'society' and who was fortunate enough to have financial security and was protected in such a way that it was impossible for them to kick all this background overboard however hard they tried. There seems to be a feeling that such a man or woman doesn't really know what it is all about; that they haven't been through the mill.

I think we have all heard the type of speaker who gets up on the platform and virtually apologizes for the fact that in spite of all their efforts, they have never attained the colorful and dramatic 'low bottom' described by the speaker who preceded them. Why should this have to be? Why should the drunk who has hit the jails, the flophouses, the state hospitals, feel that they deserve more credit for sobering up than the person who has spent years going from one private sanitarium to another, from one psychiatrist to another, in frantic efforts to arrest this illness that is common to all of us?

To my mind, the cotton wool that surrounds the rich drunk merely prolonged the agony and delayed by years the blessed release. I am sure that the miseries and horrors of coming off a drunk are very much the same, no matter where the process takes place. The walls of a suite at the Waldorf can sway and threaten to cave in, just as sickeningly as those of a cell. Those grotesque faces that creep under your eyelids are just as frightening in a penthouse as in a flophouse. Those voices whisper and threaten the same things on Park Avenue as they do on Tenth.

If the rich drunk's painful journey back to temporary health is slightly eased by good care, proper food, and sedatives, it only means that it will take them much longer to reach our common goal -- complete and permanent sobriety. They will have a few more years in which to break the hearts of their family, lose the respect of their associates, antagonize those who were their friends, and to make a complete hash of their life. As I see it, an alcoholic is an alcoholic, irrespective of color, race or creed, irrespective of the accidents of birth, money or education. So let us do away with the term: 'Park Avenue drunk' and get together in real thankfulness that we have all reached the haven of Alcoholics Anonymous.

Alcoholics Anonymous doesn't care how far down the line a person has gone in their drinking. We do not call anybody an alcoholic; we leave the decision up to them. If they say their life is disturbed and they want to do something about their drinking and are willing to accept help, they are welcomed into the fellowship of A.A. Some of us have gone much farther along the road than others, but even the so-called "sissy drinkers" are welcome if they feel that they need help. *Here is the story of a "sissy drinker":*

"The purpose of this is to offer a word of hope to the

guy or gal who may feel that they don't 'belong' in A.A. I know what it's like, for I have had the same feeling myself. Many times, the stories we hear in A.A. are about the two-fisted drinker, the guy who drank a fifth or two a day, the guy who had to have a pint anchored before he could get started, the guy who felt a binge wasn't a binge unless it lasted at least a week, the guy who could casually mention having 'done time' for drinking, the guy who spent innumerable lengths of time in hospitals or sanitariums, the guy who perhaps wound up on skid row. After listening to a few of these boys, I began to wonder if I belonged in A.A. I was a 'sissy drinker' -- of all things, a beer drinker.

My pattern had become two or three shots and beers and then I would switch to beer for the rest of the night, unless the 'edge' was too slow in coming, in which case I would help things along with a few more belts. I had never blacked out, never needed a morning drink, never been arrested, never lost a job through drinking, in fact, I never even went to a doctor, let alone a hospital or sanitarium. I still had my home, my wife and my kids, and a job, although things were shaky in the latter categories. My drinking career was over a period of about ten years. The average guy in A.A. had twenty years or more of drinking behind him, when I came into A.A. I could very easily have persuaded myself that I had ten or more years of drinking coming to me. But I wanted something when I came to A.A. and that was the answer to the question I had put to myself: 'What's wrong with the way I am drinking?' It was suggested to me that I keep coming around, keep an open mind, and decide for myself whether I was an alcoholic or not. Gradually I came to see my story in the stories of the two-fisted drinkers. Whereas one guy went out for a pack of cigarettes and came back two weeks later, I went out for a couple of hamburgers, to a tap-room of course, fully intending to take them home when they were ready, but winding up time after time getting in at five or six the next morning. Never at any time did I continue drinking into the next day. I was strictly a one-night-stand guy.

When another guy was stealing from the company he worked for in order to drink, I did it the safe way, I stole from the wife and kids. The more I came around A.A., the more I could see that I did belong; that I too was an alcoholic. By way of illustrating a point, let's say for example that I didn't feel right and went to a doctor to see what was wrong and he told me that I had a slight case of tuberculosis, but to go out and keep late hours, drink and carry on, and come back when my ailment was a little more advanced.

Such advice would make no sense whatsoever, and you would promptly go to another doctor who would tell you that since you only had a slight case, with proper rest and care, your illness would soon be arrested. You would follow the second doctor's advice because it was logical and you wanted to get well.

That is how I feel about my case of alcoholism. I was fortunate to come to A.A. when I did. I not only arrested my illness in its early stages, but saved myself untold headaches and misery, because I know today that if I had kept on drinking, I too would have eventually reached the later symptoms of alcoholism and perhaps would not get the chance to do something about it. I am grateful to God for having given me the grace to come to A.A. and even more grateful that He helped me to see that I *belonged*."

Alcoholism is a progressive illness. There is no known cure for it. But it can be arrested through following the A.A. program. Our alcoholism does not bother us as long as we stay away from the first drink. If an alcoholic stays away from alcohol their alcoholism will remain inactive and will not bother them. But if an alcoholic takes a drink even after months or years of sobriety they revert at once to their former condition. Their illness has only been arrested, not cured. Doctors have been looking for a physical cause of alcoholism for a long time, hoping to find a cure, but without success. Alcoholism is considered an illness of both the body and mind, an allergy of the body coupled with an obsession of the mind. But many feel that it is probably more a mental condition than a physical one. *The theory of a "wet subconscious" may explain why alcoholism is an incurable illness:*

"I believe that our subconscious minds will be alcoholic as long as we live. For example, I have been dry for quite a few years, yet when I am asleep I still occasionally dream that I am drunk. These dreams are a result of my wet subconscious mind. A wet subconscious may be the reason that an alcoholic is never cured, nor does it seem likely that a physical cure for alcoholism will be found, because no physical treatment can change a wet subconscious mind. When does a person become an alcoholic? When their conscious and subconscious minds have been so thoroughly conditioned that they cannot take one drink without setting in motion the mental processes that lead to drunkenness.

In A.A., we substitute a way of thinking that makes the conscious mind resistant to drinking. Our spiritual program allows the Higher Power to take over the workings of our conscious minds. But as our subconscious minds are similar to those of the lower animals, it may be impossible for a thoroughly conditioned subconscious mind to be changed from wet to dry. The theory of a wet subconscious has its advantages. It makes the A.A. program a never-ending one. With the help of God, we make a constant daily effort to keep the conscious mind in good condition, by building new walls of defense to prevent the subconscious mind from taking over. Our old way of thinking can so often leap from the subconscious to the conscious. We must be very careful about daydreaming and wishful thinking.

The theory of the wet subconscious also explains slips, which sometimes occur even after several years of sobriety. The thoughts that come before taking a drink are often largely subconscious. The person usually doesn't know consciously what made them do it. Our subconscious minds may never become free from alcoholic thoughts as long as we live but when, through our spiritual program, our conscious minds are fully conditioned against drinking, we can stay sober and our subconscious minds do not often bother us.

We shudder when a person says: 'I'll never take another drink as long as I live.' How do they know? Their wet subconscious mind is always there, ready to take over if they ever let down the bars of their conscious dry thinking.

An idle thought connected with drinking casually pops into my mind. This is the crucial moment. Will I harbor that thought even for one minute, or will I banish it from my mind at once? If I let it stay, it may develop into a daydream. If I allow the daydream to stay in my mind it may lead to a decision, however unconscious, to take a drink. Then I am headed for a slip. As long as we live, we must be on the lookout for such thoughts and guard against them. In fact, our A.A. spiritual training is largely to prepare us for this eventuality, to make us able to recognize such thoughts at once and to reject them at once.

The A.A. program is largely one of spiritual training. With the help of God, we must fill our minds with constructive thoughts. The length of our sobriety is not as important as the quality of it. A person who has been a member of A.A. for a number of years may not be in as good spiritual condition as a person who has only been in a few months. We must realize that as long as we live, we are only one drink away from a drunk.

Temptation comes as a result of our neglect of the spiritual program of constructive thinking to such an extent that the wet subconscious has a chance to take over the dry conscious mind. The theory of the wet subconscious is nothing to be discouraged about. It simply means that we must practice the A.A. principles in all our affairs as long as we live. This means regular attendance at A.A. meetings, no graduation from A.A., no diplomas, no overconfidence and no letting down the spiritual control of our character defects which, if allowed, will weaken our conscious control and allow the wet subconscious to take over."

Many people can "drink like ladies and gentlemen," hold their liquor and feel no after-craving for a drink. We in Alcoholics Anonymous are not prohibitionists. We do not wish to deprive those persons who can handle their liquor. A.A. has nothing to offer to these normal drinkers. There exists no liquor problem for them. We can only wish more power to them; may they always be able to control their drinking.

Our program is for those to whom alcohol has become a problem -- the true, heart-weary, ego-inflated, defeated alcoholic. If a man or woman is sincerely desirous of obtaining sobriety to the exclusion of all other wishes or ideas, and is fully willing to not only admit but accept the fact that he or she is an alcoholic and that his or her life has become unmanageable, in other words to take the first step in our program, they are welcome to join our fellowship.

The only requirement for membership in Alcoholics Anonymous is an honest desire to stop drinking. After a few months in A.A., our sobriety becomes the most important thing in our lives. We know that it must always be kept in first place in our thinking. *We believe in:*

First Things First.

2. FELLOWSHIP

Live and Let Live

Only an alcoholic wholly understands another alcoholic. That is why Alcoholics Anonymous has been so successful. Doctors, ministers and psychiatrists often throw up their hands and admit that they have very little success in helping the alcoholic to sober up. The alcoholic will seldom accept advice from a doctor, a minister, a priest or a psychiatrist, who feel that since they are not alcoholics, have not suffered what they have suffered, that they do not understand. Therefore, alcoholics often fail to cooperate with them when they offer their services.

The illness of alcoholism is baffling, frustrating and discouraging to those who try to help the sufferer. But alcoholics who are members of A.A. can be uniquely useful people. They can help an alcoholic whereas somebody who has not had their experience with drinking could not help them. An alcoholic will usually accept help from another alcoholic, because they know that the other alcoholic has been through the same things that they have and knows what they are talking about. One alcoholic understands another.

Here is a quotation from the book, *Alcoholics Anonymous:* "For most normal folks drinking means conviviality, companionship, and colorful imagination. It means release from care, boredom, and worry. It is joyous intimacy with friends and a feeling that life is good. But not so with us. In those last days of heavy drinking, the old pleasures were gone. They were but memories. Never could we recapture the great moments of the past. There was an insistent yearning to enjoy life as we once did and a heart-breaking obsession that some new miracle of control would enable us to do it. There was always one more attempt and one more failure.

The less people tolerated us, the more we withdrew from society, from life itself. As we became subjects of King Alcohol, shivering denizens of his mad realm, the chilling vapor that is loneliness settled down. It thickened, ever becoming blacker. Some of us sought out sordid places, hoping to find understanding companionship and approval. Momentarily we did, then would come oblivion and the awful awakening to face the hideous Four Horsemen: Terror, Bewilderment, Frustration and Despair. Some day the alcoholic will be unable to imagine life either with alcohol or without it. Then he will know loneliness such as few do. He will be at the jumping-off place. He will wish for the end.

When offered the A.A. program, he may say: 'Yes, I'm willing. But am I to be consigned to a life where I shall be stupid, boring, and glum, like some righteous people I see? I know I must get along without liquor, but how can I? Have you a sufficient substitute?' Yes, there is a substitute and it is vastly more than that. It is the fellowship of Alcoholics Anonymous. There you will find release from care, boredom and worry. Your imagination will be fired. Life will mean something at last. The most satisfactory years of your existence lie ahead. Thus we find the fellowship and so will you."

Members of Alcoholics Anonymous form groups for mutual help and understanding. These groups meet once or twice a week, where speakers are heard and discussions are held. *Here is a description of what the A.A. meeting means to us:*

"In a large measure, the meeting is the key to A.A.'s phenomenal and unprecedented success. The meeting is a much more effective persuader and convincer than a book or a pamphlet. It is practically impossible to learn to swim by reading a book, or to drive a car, run a large corporation, or converse fluently in a modern language by reading a book. You have to get into the water, sit behind the wheel, beat your way up the economic ladder, live among foreigners and listen to the music of their inflection and cadence. A.A. is like that in many respects.

The meeting has a two-fold effect upon those who attend with an open mind and the right attitude. First of all, it makes a direct intellectual appeal. The A.A. member sits in the audience and listens. He is not on the psychiatrist's couch and does not have to say a word. He can admit anything and everything to himself, but he need not tell anyone in the world about it. At least, not tonight. He may agree with the speaker or think silently to himself: 'That's the bunk. It's really like this ....' In his act of agreement or disagreement, he is beginning to think constructively about alcohol, himself and the A.A. His process of mental recovery is under way.

Over a series of meetings, cases are cited, principles enunciated, philosophies evolved. Clashes of opinion may occur, but they are provocative of thought. Which of the two views is correct? An answer may occupy a member for days, but during that period he will be thinking in a way and in an area completely new to him. His errors, prejudices, resentments fade and shrivel in the light of group experience and the warmth of group therapy.

It is the action of mind upon mind in the meetings, open or closed, that provides the mental exercise and experienced guidance which the befogged mind needs for recovery. The great contribution of the meeting, however, is probably not intellectual at all. It is more indirect, more subtle.

The late Justice Bradeis once said that he was convinced that good health was contagious, just as disease was contagious. Surely, conditions of mind are even more contagious than those of the body. We know moods--gloom, laughter--are contagious. Mental sobriety too is contagious and can be contracted at an A.A. meeting. The new member whose thinking is twisted is thrown in with others well along the road to recovery. He somehow 'catches on,' just as the boy 'gets the hang' of swimming by splashing around in the water with companions who can swim. A solid grounding in A.A., a sane outlook on life, a reasonable amount of serenity, and a fair share of all the fruits of the A.A. program can be had at an A.A. meeting." *Here is how a typical A.A. meeting is run:*

"For the benefit of newcomers and visitors, the leader should open the meeting with a clear, concise statement of what A.A. is--and what it is not! That A.A. is not affiliated with any group, political opinion, moral issue, religious organization; that it takes no sides on public questions; that its sole object is to help those alcoholics who want help; that we have no dues, no pledges, no initiation fees, no axes to grind. This opening procedure not only identifies the purpose of the meeting, but provides a back-drop for the speakers who follow. Thus, their individual remarks and opinions are from the very outset related to the larger purpose of A.A. as a whole.

Either tacked onto this opening statement or very early in the meeting, the leader should also explain that the A.A. program is based on our twelve suggested steps. Some groups read the steps verbatim. Others less formally explain them in the leader's own words. In either event, it's impor-tant. For it indicates that while we have no organization, no constitution, no bylaws, we do have a central core of belief, a definite program of recovery and rehabilitation. It is the leader's responsibility to choose his speakers with an eye to 'balance.'

Using as our example the three-speaker type of program so popular in most sections of the country, the three selected should never be all of the 'showy type.' They may make your meeting sound professional. A.A. is not founded on oratory, but on humble, sometimes stumbling, efforts. Nor should all three speakers be strongly spiritual in their talk. Such a concentration can make the program sound like a church, perhaps even a mission, to the new-comer. And no matter how deeply we may feel about A.A.'s spirituality, we are duty bound to remember that the new-comer is apt to be God-shy at first.

For similar reasons, all the speakers should not be 'comedians' either. A good belly-laugh here and there is a priceless ingredient. But a meeting of unrelieved hilarity merely makes A.A. look silly and inconsequential.

Last but not least, the speakers should never be all of the same type, neither all from 'skid row' nor 'silk-stocking.' It is our job to make each meeting, as far as is practicable a true cross-section of people (which A.A. is) and a cross-section of opinion (which A.A. has), so as to give the newcomer the widest possible opportunity to identify himself or herself with us.

Speakers should be introduced briefly, without excessive fanfare. The leader should comment between speakers, but not by amplifying what the previous speaker has just said, in any way that sounds like 'What Joe meant to say was ....' All that can accomplish is to make Joe look like a moron. If the third and final speaker has not already done so, the leader before closing should sum up the entire meeting, relating what has been said to the aims and purposes set forth in the opening statement, sort of tying the whole thing into one neat package for the newcomer to take away with him. Then the leader should invite newcomers and visitors to come back to subsequent meetings, pointing out that while this has been a typical meeting, it is far from being a complete conception of the A.A. program.

Only continued attendance and a variety of meetings can convey the full meaning of the A.A. way of life. All A.A. meetings conclude with the universal custom, recitation of the Lord's Prayer, in which the leader invites all to join in."

The way of Alcoholics Anonymous is the way of fellowship. People were not made to live alone. A hermit's life is not a normal or natural one. We all need to be by ourselves at times, but we cannot really live without the companionship of others. Our natures demand it. Our lives depend largely upon it. The fellowship of A.A. seems to us to be the best in the world, because it is real.

Our drinking fellowship was a substitute one for lack of something better. At the time, we did not realize what real fellowship could be. Drinking fellowship has a fatal fault. It is not based on a firm foundation. Most of it is on the surface. It is based mostly on the desire to use your companions for your own pleasure and using others is a false foundation. Drinking fellowship has been praised in song and story. The "cup that cheers" has become famous as a means of companionship. But when we realize that the higher centers of our brains are dulled or paralyzed by alcohol, we know that such fellowship cannot be on the highest plane. It is at best only a substitute for real fellowship.

Doctors think of the A.A. fellowship as "group therapy." This is a very narrow conception of the depth of the A.A. fellowship. Looking at it merely as a means of acquiring and holding sobriety, it is right as far as it goes. But it doesn't go far enough. Group therapy is directed toward the help that the individual receives from it. It is essentially selfish. It is using the companionship of other alcoholics only in order to stay sober ourselves. But this is only the beginning of real A.A. fellowship.

Clergymen speak of the spiritual fellowship of the church members. This is much closer to the A.A. fellowship than mere group therapy. Such fellowship is based on a common belief in God and a common effort to live a spiritual life. We try to do this in A.A., but we also try to get down into the real problems in each other's lives. We try to really open up to each other. We have a real desire to be of service to each other. We try to go down deep into the personal lives of our members.

We come now to the A.A. fellowship. It is partly group therapy. It is partly spiritual fellowship. But it is even more. It is based on a common illness, a common failure, and a common problem. It goes down deep into our personal lives and our personal needs. It requires a full opening up to each other of our inmost thoughts and most secret problems. All barriers between us are swept aside. They have to to be. Then we try to help each other get well. The A.A. fellowship is based on a sincere desire to help the other fellow. In A.A. we can be sure of sympathy, understanding, and real help. These things make the A.A. fellowship the best that we know.

Of course, our A.A. members enter into the fellowship of A.A. in varying degrees. Some are more or less reluctant or passive. Others are happy and even joyous. *The joyous ones are the real "rocks of A.A."*

"All members of Alcoholics Anonymous who are honest with themselves are sober. Some of them are reluctantly sober. Others are passively sober. Some are happily sober. Others are joyously sober. Why is there a difference? It's the quality of their sobriety. Sober is sober, you may say. If a guy or a gal isn't drinking, then he's sober, that's all there is to it. But that isn't all there is to it. A ride on the waterwagon will bring sobriety, at least for the duration of the ride. But it's likely to be a pretty low grade of sobriety. It's a reluctant sobriety, the 'I-don't-like-this-but-I've-got-to' kind. The rider is so sorry for himself that he won't even talk to the driver. He might just as well be going through a tunnel, for all the passing scene means to him. Some members of A.A. are like that.

Then there's the passive sobriety. This alcoholic has reached the bottom below which he doesn't want to go, so he joins A.A. He comes to meetings, listens a bit, talks a bit, puts enough of the principles to work to keep himself sober, takes only a passive interest in the group, seldom has time for twelfth-step work, absorbs as much as he needs and gives only what is brushed from him through contact. He's sober, yes. But he isn't the kind of member that has made A.A. grow, that has enabled A.A. to reach out to the thousands of hopeless drunks and restore them to sanity. He isn't particularly happy or unhappy. He's rather numb about the whole thing. Fortunately there aren't too many members like him.

Then there's the happy type of sobriety. This fellow accepts defeat. He knows that he and liquor don't get along and he takes hold of A.A. with enthusiasm. He seems to grasp the program quickly and shows he is putting it to work. He enters into group affairs and carries his share or more than his share of the load. He attends meetings. He does twelfth-step work as it comes and hunts for more. He tends to be a little evangelistic at the start, later cools off as he gains experience and becomes a solid member of the group. He's pretty happy about the whole thing. He's changed the pattern of his life and his associations. And while occasionally he may long momentarily for the good old days when liquor was fun, before it became a problem to him, he doesn't brood about it and he's fairly well satisfied with his lot. Many members stay in this class throughout their association with the fellowship. But a great many more stay in this group only for a while, then slip almost unnoticed into another classification.

This last group is the one which enjoys a joyous sobriety. Those who are blessed with joyous sobriety can't be separated physically from the happily sober ones. No halo hangs over their heads. No particular gleam sparkles from their eyes. Theirs is an inward joyousness that stems from gratitude to a gracious God who has selected them from the great mass of alcoholics for special consideration, a God who might have picked any one of thousands of hopeless drunks, but instead elected to present them with the gift of sobriety. These joyous A.A.s are humble folk, who know that humility consists not in groveling but in having a true perspective of their spiritual assets and liabilities. These are the members to whom others refer as having achieved serenity, although they'd be the first to deny it. Their lives aren't serene but they have achieved the ability to take things as they come, to roll with the punches, to change those things they can and to ask the God of their understanding for guidance and counsel in all things.

These are the folks who started doing for others because they were told they should, that it was part of the program. But as they grew spiritually, they found that in direct proportion to the amount of good they did willingly and freely, with no thought of recompense, the good things of life both spiritually and materially were returned to them. Soon they needed no reason for doing good. They now just do it as a part of decent living. They live a day at a time, placing themselves in the hands of a Higher Power each morning to carry out His will for that day; to ask daily to be so filled with His grace that it can be passed on to others. In doing these things, they don't think of themselves as anything special. They do only what they think in their hearts they should. We all know them. While they give no outward indication, they stand out everywhere. They're the rocks with which the temple of A.A. has slowly risen. We can all be like them, if only we will put forth the effort. It is up to us."

A.A. members strive to be grateful, humble and tolerant. They try to keep in a grateful frame of mind. If they achieve a true estimate of their own worth, they are humble. Self-respect is entirely compatible with the A.A. type of humility. We are tolerant. *We believe in* :

Live and Let Live.

3. SURRENDER

But for the Grace of God

Since an alcoholic cannot stop drinking by their own will power, they must turn to a Power greater than themselves. The way of A.A. is the way of faith in a Power greater than ourselves, whom most of us call God, who can give us the strength we need to get well.

We don't get the full benefit of the A.A. program until we surrender our lives to some Power greater than ourselves and trust that Power to give us the strength we need. There is no better way for us. We can get sober without it. We can stay sober for some time without it. But if we are going to truly live, we must take *the way of faith*. That is the path for us. We must follow it if we want real peace. The way of faith is of course not confined to A.A. It is the way for everybody who wants to really live. But many people can go through life without much of it. Many are doing so, to their own sorrow.

But for us in A.A. the way of faith is the way of life. We have proved by our past lives that we could not live without it. Unless we have the key of faith to unlock the meaning of life, we are lost. We do not choose faith because it is one way for us, but because it is the only way. We cannot live victoriously without faith. We are at sea without a rudder to steer us or an anchor to hold us, drifting on the sea of life. Wayfarers without a home.

Our souls are restless until they find rest in God.

Without faith, our lives are a meaningless succession of unrelated happenings, without rhyme or reason. When we surrender our lives to God, we are at home and at rest.

The Second Step in our A.A. program is "Came to believe that a Power greater than ourselves could restore us to sanity." The Third Step is: "Made a decision to turn our will and our lives over to the care of God *as we understood Him.*" We put our drink problem in the hands of God and leave it there. We do not reach out and take the problem back into our own hands. We leave it in God's hands. We surrender our lives to God. We put our lives, with all our problems and difficulties, all our failures and defeats, into God's care. Our faith should control the whole of our lives.

We alcoholics were living divided lives. We had to find a way to make them whole. When we were drinking, our lives were made up of a lot of scattered and unrelated pieces. We must pick up our lives and put them together again. We do this by recovering faith in that Divine Principle in the universe which holds us together and holds the whole universe together and gives it meaning and purpose. We surrender our disorganized lives to that Power, we get in harmony with the Divine Spirit, and our lives are made whole again.

We in A.A. believe in prayer. We have a little prayer which we all use and which we think is especially appropriate to the alcoholic: *"God grant me the serenity to accept the things I cannot change, the courage to change the things I can, and the wisdom to know the difference."* This is known as the Serenity Prayer and is used universally throughout A.A.

This timeless little prayer has been credited to almost every theologian, philosopher and saint known to man. It was actually written by Dr. Reinhold Niebuhr of Union Theological Seminary, New York City, in about 1932, as the ending to a longer prayer. In 1934, the Doctor's friend and neighbor, Dr. Howard Robbins, asked permission to use that part of the longer prayer in a compilation he was making at the time. It was published in that year in Dr. Robbins' book of prayers. Dr. Niebuhr says: "Of course, it may have been around for years, even centuries, but I don't think so. I honestly do believe that I wrote it myself." It came to the attention of an early member of A.A. in 1939. He read it in an obituary notice appearing in *The New York Times.* He liked it so much that he brought it to the A.A. office on Vesey Street for Bill W. to read. When Bill and the others read this little prayer, they felt that it particularly suited the needs of the members of Alcoholics Anonymous. Cards were printed and passed around. Thus this simple little prayer became an integral part of the A.A. movement. Today it is in the pockets of thousands of A.A.s. It is framed and placed on the walls of A.A. meeting rooms throughout the world. We A.A.s believe that "the things I cannot change" are mostly outside of ourselves, while "the things I can" are mostly within ourselves.

Many clergymen are enthusiastic about the A.A. movement. *The following tribute was written by a non-alcoholic clergyman:*

"God in His wisdom selected you men and women to be the purveyors of His goodness. In selecting you, through whom to bring about this phenomenon, He went not to the proud, the mighty, the famous, or the brilliant. He went to the humble, the sick, the unfortunate. He went right to the drunkard, the so-called weakling of the world.

Well might He have said to you: 'Unto your weak and feeble hands I have entrusted a power beyond estimate. To you has been given that which has been denied to the most learned of your fellows. Not to scientists or statesmen, not to wives or mothers, not even to My priests or ministers have I given this gift of healing other alcoholics, which I entrust to you.

It must be used unselfishly. It carries with it grave responsibility. No day can be too long, no demands upon your time too urgent, no case too pitiful, no task too hard, no effort too great. It must be used with tolerance for I have restricted its application to no race, no creed, no denomination.

Personal criticism you must expect, lack of appreciation will be common, ridicule will sometimes be your lot, your motives may sometimes be misjudged. You must be prepared for adversity, for what men call adversity is the ladder you must use to ascend towards spiritual perfection. And remember that in the exercise of this power I shall not exact of you beyond your capabilities.

You are not selected because of exceptional talents. Be careful always, if success attends your efforts, not to ascribe to your personal superiority that to which you can lay claim only by virtue of My gift. If I had wanted learned men to accomplish this mission, the power would have been

entrusted to the physician and the scientist. If I had wanted
eloquent men, there would have been many anxious for the
assignment, for talk is the easiest used of all talents with
which I have endowed mankind. If I had wanted scholarly
men, the world is filled with better qualified men than you,
who would be available.

You were selected because you have been outcasts
of the world and your long experience as drunkards has
made you humbly alert to the cries of distress that come
from the lonely hearts of alcoholics everywhere."

Many Catholic priests are also enthusiastic about the
A.A. movement. *The following tribute was written by a Jesuit:*

"If you have ever been inclined to snicker when you
heard the words 'Alcoholics Anonymous,' you owe a lot of
people an apology. Thousands have come to scoff and
remained to pray. We have often heard about these A.A.
groups, but is just recently that we have had occasion to take
an active interest in their undertakings. It may sound like a
Hollywood press release but 'terrific' was the word that
came to mind when we fully realized what they are doing.

Here indeed is the rejected cornerstone become the
keystone of the building. Here is an example of the impossible become possible. The A.A. makes no bones about con-
ceding what he was. A rummy, a bum, a derelict, a no-good
down-and-outer. An alcoholic's life runs along as though
cut to a pattern. In some cases, the dip from normality and
respectability to abnormality, degradation and disgrace is a
sudden one. In most cases it is a gradual descent from sane
living to a slow enslavement to drink. Once the thin thread

that separates the 'social' drinker from the alcoholic is broken, there is no fool-proof remedy known to the medical profession that can cure the illness. The usual spiritual remedies are at best a temporary relief.

The non-alcoholic world has never been able to penetrate the alcoholic mind successfully. But the groups that are now known as 'Alcoholics Anonymous' have performed that miracle and their success is increasingly astounding. If you are not familiar with their therapy and technique, you will find it the most intriguing study you have entered upon. Two things stand out, *first,* there are no half-way measures, it is all or nothing, and *second*, the approach is so basically sound and so soundly spiritual that you will say without hesitation: 'The finger of God is here!'

The alcoholic who is really determined to quit gives himself to God completely, without cavil, without reservation. He follows it up with a graduated program, consisting of twelve spiritual steps. He's 'in' and he knows it. For the rest of his life, his one all-consuming purpose is to stay 'in.' He does that by becoming an apostle to other alcoholics. Analyze it as you like. Question it. Scoff at it. Say: 'It's impossible.'

The simple fact is that it works and it does the job as no one else, no other agency, has been able to do it. The reason? One--the candidate for A.A. must throw himself into the arms of God, as he understands God. Two--he makes it a day-to-day, twenty-four hour struggle to stay in God's grace and presence. Three--he aims to make any sacrifice to share his new-found blessing with another alco-

holic in need of help. The social and spiritual security of
every single member is bound up with the welfare of all.

This is social action with a capital 'S.' A.A. is not a
religion; it is the basis for a *new way of life*. It insists upon and
stresses the absolute need of spiritual principles in life. It
encourages each member to follow his own faith, or to find
a faith if he has none. It neither commends nor condemns
any man's religious beliefs. Controversy is completely and
entirely outside its field and scope . . . like any human
organization, there are degrees of success and execution of
the program. Some stand out more prominently than
others.

There is no doubt in our mind that the active A.A.
member displays an apostolic spirit of self-sacrifice that is
reminiscent of the early Christians. The movement is built
on humility, honesty, courage, charity, complete faith and
trust in God, a deliberate surrender of self to the Supreme
Being. How could it fail? How could it be anything else but
progressively successful? Active membership in Alcoholics
Anonymous is a hard-won badge of honor, worthy of the
admiration of all. This is a leaven with a limitless potential.
It must be dear to the heart of God . . ."

We in Alcoholics Anonymous believe in having a
quiet time in the morning before breakfast. We read a little,
pray a little, meditate a while. We try to get our minds in the
right condition for the day. We ask God to help us today to
live the way He wants us to live. We pray that His will be
done, through us. We ask Him for the strength to stay away
from one drink for one day. We also pray during the day,

whenever we feel the need of prayer to help us to face things. Our most-used prayer is "Thy will be done." Underneath us are the Everlasting Arms. We do not have to face life alone--ever again. *Here is a little story about a spiritual experience:*

"A man went into a church one day, walked down the aisle, knelt at the altar, looked up at the Cross, immediately arose and left. He did this every day for a week. The sexton noticed this and told the pastor. The pastor watched the man for several days, then his curiosity getting the best of him, he stopped the visitor and asked: 'I'm not trying to pry into your affairs, but you have been coming here every day for the past ten or twelve days, about the same time, walking down the aisle, kneeling at the altar, looking up at the Cross, and immediately getting up and leaving. You are not there long enough to pray. We thought you might be stealing money which the worshippers leave at the altar, but we know now that you are not doing that. If you don't mind, how about telling us what's taking place?'

'No, sir, I don't mind,' the fellow replied. 'You see, it's like this. I'm an alcoholic. About a month ago I joined a fellowship known as Alcoholics Anonymous. They have twelve suggested steps, and eleven of them are spiritual. Knowing very little about God, and nothing at all about prayer, each day when I get off from work, I enter your church, walk down the aisle, kneel at the altar, look up at the Cross and say: "God, this is Jim."' The fellow came in a few more days and then they began to miss him. Several weeks later, the pastor, while on his rounds of the hospital went into the accident ward and was talking to the boys there, when one said: 'See that fellow over in the corner bed? He's been here a week now and seems very despondent. Undoubtedly he hasn't a family, for no one has been here to see him. How about going over and seeing if you can cheer him up?'

When the pastor approached the bed, who was there but Jim, with the most beautiful expression he had ever seen on a man's face. He was astonished and said: 'Jim, the boys asked me to come over and cheer you up, but your face is so radiant that it cheers me. And they say there has been no one here to see you.' 'Oh yes,' Jim said, 'I had a visitor.' The pastor looked perplexed. 'But the boys insisted that no one has been here.' 'But they were wrong,' Jim said. 'About an hour ago I had a visitor. He stood right at the foot of the bed.' The pastor asked: 'Did the visitor talk to you?' 'Yes,' said Jim. 'What did he say?' He said, 'Jim, this is God."

We in A.A. believe that we have recovered through the grace of God. "But for the Grace of God" we would still be drinking. When we see another alcoholic in the condition that we were in, our hearts go out to them, and we say to ourselves: "But for the Grace of God, there go I."

These words of John Bradford, English Protestant martyr, are a familiar motto in nearly every clubroom where A.A. group meetings are in session. Four centuries ago, in 1552 A.D., the pastor of London's St. Paul's Church is supposed to have said: "But for the Grace of God, there goes John Bradford," whenever he saw evil-doers taken to jail.

To members of Alcoholics Anonymous, the phrase has come to have a broader meaning. To the newcomer in A.A., the words may well mean: "But for the Grace of God, I would still be drinking. I would not have found A.A." To the old timer in A.A., the words may well mean: "By God's grace I have attained and maintained sobriety. I am making progress in growth along the lines suggested in the program of recovery."

To A.A.s who volunteer to carry the message of A.A. inside prison walls, John Bradford's words have an obvious and special meaning that makes it a special privilege to extend the helping hand of A.A. to those now behind steel bars, who on release are determined never again to be in front of mahogany bars.

For all, there is grace along the twelve-step way, that grace which is the influence of God operating in people to regenerate them or to strengthen them. *Truly, when we see a fellow alcoholic suffering as we did, we can say with deep feeling:*

But for the Grace of God.

4. INVENTORY

Keep an Open Mind

In order for the alcoholic to get the full benefit of the A.A. program, they must get rid of the blocks that are keeping them from a new way of life. These blocks are mostly our defects of character. To quote the book, *Alcoholics Anonymous:*

"Those who do not recover are people who are constitutionally incapable of being honest with themselves. There are such unfortunates. They are not at fault. They seem to be born that way. They are naturally incapable of grasping and developing a manner of living which demands rigorous honesty. Their chances are less than average. There are those too who suffer from grave emotional and mental disorders, but many of them do recover if they have the capacity to be honest .

We who have accepted the A.A. principles have all been faced with the necessity for a thorough personal housecleaning. We must face and be rid of the things in ourselves which have been blocking us. We therefore take a personal inventory. We take stock honestly. We search out the flaws in our make-up which caused our failure.

Resentment is the number one offender. Life which includes deep resentment leads only to futility and unhappiness. If we are to live, we must be free of anger. When we saw our faults, we listed them. We placed them before us in black and white. We admitted our wrongs honestly and we were willing to set these matters straight.

We reviewed our fears thoroughly. We asked God to remove these fears, and we commenced to outgrow fear. Many of us needed an overhauling in regard to sex. We came to believe that sex powers were God-given and therefore good if used properly. Sex is never to be used lightly or selfishly, nor is it to be despised or loathed. If sex is troublesome, we throw ourselves the harder into helping others, and so take our minds off ourselves.

Unless we discuss our defects with another person, we do not acquire enough humility, fearlessness and honesty. We must be entirely honest with somebody, if we expect to live happily in this world. We must be hard on ourselves, but always considerate of others.

If we are still clinging to something that we will not let go, we must sincerely ask God to help us to be willing to let even that go. We cannot divide our lives into compartments and keep some compartments for ourselves. We must give all the compartments to God. We should say: 'My Creator, I am now willing that You should have all of me, good and bad. I pray that you now remove from me every single defect of character which stands in the way of my usefulness to You and to my fellows.'"

In taking our inventory, we look at ourselves as we really are. And we also face our alcoholic problem. We look at it objectively, and consider the real cost of taking a drink. *Here are the thoughts of a man who considers the price of a drink too high:*

"I've been thinking of all it would cost me if I took a drink today. I find that the longer I go without a drink, the greater the cost of one drink would be.

If I take a drink today, I'll get into my room at the Y.M.C.A. some time after the bars close tonight, fairly drunk, because I won't take just one drink. And about seven tomorrow morning I'll get up, feeling rotten and wanting a drink.

After the drink and a cup of coffee, I'll go to work, feeling guilty and nervous and with a foggy brain. I'll probably struggle through the day, but certainly no later than five P.M., and then I'll head for a bar--*if I take a drink today.*

The next night I'll be so drunk that I'll be afraid to go into the Y.M.C.A. (I almost got kicked out of there before), so when the bars close I'll end up in a high-priced room in a hotel. On the third or fourth day, I'll still be at the hotel, paying exorbitant prices for things I don't need. The bellboy on the way up to my room with a drink will meet another on the way down with empty glasses. For as long as the money holds out, the drinks will keep coming--*if I take a drink today.*

By this time, I'll be very nervous and concerned about avoiding people I know. Things will run along like this for several days, until the supply of dollars I have in my pocket now will have dwindled to only a few. Those of you whom I may have met and who might have tried to pull me out of it, will have given up and I will be entirely alone. My wife, from the absence of mail from me, will know what has happened and all the confidence she has built up in me these past several months will be gone--*if I take a drink today.*

Realization of these things will only cause me to drink more and faster and within a couple of weeks after that first drink, I'll have moved to cheaper quarters and soon my funds will all be gone and I'll start borrowing--ten here, five there at first, then two and one, until I can't borrow any more--*if I take a drink today.*

Then I'll begin sneaking into the Y.M.C.A. to get things to pawn, first my radio, which I enjoy so much and which I had a hell of a time getting out last time, then one suit and then another, until there is nothing left but what I have on my back--*if I take a drink today.*

From here on, it is hard to predict just what will happen. I may get a job in a restaurant, or I may go back to my old job at a reduced salary. Or I may have a commitment to Kalamazoo hanging over my head, or be in jail for 30, 60, or 90 days-*if I take a drink today.*

But at the very best, I can only be back at work under reduced earnings and restrictions. I doubt that I'll have my room at the Y.M.C.A. I'll have all those debts to pay back, including a doctor's bill. What clothes I have left will be too large, for the fifteen pounds I have gained in the past few months will have been consumed in alcohol. All those whom I can now call friends will be skeptical at best and with very good reason to be--*if I take a drink today.*

However, regardless of what kind of recovery I might make, with the things I absolutely know it will cost me--*the price is just too great.* I know it will cost me every dollar I have now and what I can borrow, in addition to loss of income. I know I'll suffer the pangs of hell, wherever I am, both mentally and physically. I know I'll lose the respect and encouragement of my wife and my employers and associates will speak and think of me in terms of doubt--*if I take a drink today.*

Since I've been sober, a lot of good things have happened to me which would not have happened if I had taken a drink. My wife has spent a grand two weeks' vacation with me--the first time we've been together for six years. My brother and his wife have been here to visit me-- the first time in nine years. And I've had a week's vacation with pay at the boss' cottage with my wife.

I've seen several good ball games, a couple of cir- cuses and numerous other things I enjoy, none of which would have happened--*if I took a drink*. My wife is ready to come to Grand Rapids and make a home for me any time it can be arranged and the future in general looks brighter for me than in many years.

So you see, the price of a drink does get greater with the passing of each day of sobriety. I don't know how nearly parallel my case may run with any of yours, but certainly close enough so that none of you can afford to pay the price of a drink today, if you are an alcoholic.

If you are an alcoholic, take a tip from one who is, *you can't take a drink today* any more than I can, without getting drunk and into trouble. So, summing it all up and adding it backwards and forwards, the answer is the same--the price is just too great *if I take a drink today*."

We alcoholics are emotional people. We have our swings from elation to depression. Many of our upsets come from our lack of emotional control. *Here are the thoughts of a man who is seeking to escape from his emotional bondage:*

"My wife and I were homeward bound from a Satur- day night social visit with other A.A. friends. I had been silent most of the evening, sunk in one of my periodic depressed spells, speaking only when absolutely necessary, as on other similar occasions. I had been sober about eighteen months at the time I write about.

There was no desire to drink, but emotionally I was swinging like the man on the flying trapeze. My moody spells in A.A. must finally have taxed the patience of my non-alcoholic wife, because she threw caution aside and began to talk about them, as we rode along. She asked me if I had ever stopped to realize that mental depressions had been part of my previous drinking pattern, as well as recurring spells of boredom. She also ventured the opinion that some alcoholics seemed to get drunk emotionally, before they got drunk alcoholically.

Being furious, and startled, I checked an impulse to yell at her, thinking silently instead that a non-alcoholic ought to mind her own business. Several weeks passed before I grudgingly realized that my sobriety was part of her business. She too had a stake in it. If I got drunk again, as in pre-A.A. days, she also would lose by it. This self-inventory continued and the more I probed into my alcoholic past, the surer became the conviction that she had put her finger on the weakest link in my efforts to work the A.A. program, with wisdom and happiness.

One fact, above all others, revealed itself most glaringly. It was inescapable and beyond doubt. All during my alcoholism and continuing through my early A.A. sobriety, I had experienced periodically what I have identified as emotional circles. It was a definite and positive pattern of thought and behavior which had in the past, and would again in the future, unless checked, lead inevitably to the first drink. It was and still is the second most important discovery that I've made about myself in A.A.

The first, of course, was that I am an alcoholic. You might be interested and helped by knowing how my emotional circle (or cycle) used to repeat itself every few months. When I was perched on top of it (happy), I was a good Joe, easy to satisfy, pleasant and amiable, and at peace with myself and the world. Then slowly, imperceptibly at first, I began to slide down one side of my circle. I got tense. Little things magnified themselves. Nothing pleased me. Finally I reached the place where everything looked drab and sour. Now I was at the bottom of my circle (mental depression, boredom, or both).

My daily mood was a deep, dark pit of self-pity, resentments, and hopelessness. I was ripe again emotionally for the first drink. After many days of miserable existence, one of two things happened; either I managed to fight my way out of it, or nature did it for me. I began to climb the other side of my emotional circle and on reaching the top, I was a happy and contented man once more.

If you have been similarly bewildered and bedeviled by a recurring emotional circle in your life, especially one which makes you unable to live satisfactorily with yourself or others, why not begin now to do something about it, in order to make the practice of your sobriety much easier? Otherwise, you will continue, as I did, to descend and ascend like an elevator.

In anything like chronic or periodic emotionalism, there are always warning symptoms before the circle starts to operate, before our pleasant or happy mood begins to change, preparatory to another plunge into misery and the feeling of hopelessness. Learn how to detect the beginning of an impending change in yourself. Fight harder each time to stay longer on top of your emotional circle.

Perhaps, like me, you'll fail for a while to hold onto your happy mood. But practice makes perfect in most things and you'll eventually succeed in your purpose. No A.A., suffering in this respect, need remain a captive in his or her emotional bondage.

If mental depression, boredom, or any other kind of emotionalism is an enemy to your peace of mind, there is an escape for you. But the effort to free ourselves of extreme emotional ups and downs must start with a knowledge of ourselves, why we blow hot and cold about our sobriety, the program, or anything else, and with doing something about it right at the beginning of such an attack and not delaying until we're in the middle of another emotional fermentation."

The Fourth Step in our A.A. program is: "Made a searching and fearless moral inventory of ourselves." The Fifth Step is "Admitted to God, to ourselves, and to another human being, the exact nature of our wrongs." The Sixth Step: "Were entirely ready to have God remove all those defects of character." The Seventh Step: "Humbly asked Him to remove our shortcomings." When we have taken these steps, we can start over again with a clean slate. We are free from the blocks which were keeping us from a new way of life.

Now we need to make a daily check-up of our faults, in order to keep ourselves in the proper spiritual condition.

By following the A.A. program, we gradually increase our insight into our defects of character. Our blindness to our own faults slowly leaves us. We learn to recognize them and gradually eliminate them from our lives. Our spiritual growth is not so much reaching for the things of God, but of removing blocks, so that the spirit of God can reach our hearts.

When a man or woman comes to an A.A. meeting, he or she is not just coming into a meeting, but into a new way of life. We are always impressed by the change we see in people after they've been in A.A. for a while. Every once in a while we should take an inventory of ourselves, to see whether we have changed and if so, in what way. Before we met A.A., we were very *selfish*.

We wanted our own way in everything. We never grew up. When things went wrong, we sulked like spoiled children and usually went out and got drunk. We were all get and no give. Before we met A.A., we were very *dishonest*.

We lied constantly about where we had been and what we'd been doing. We took time off from our jobs and pretended we'd been sick or gave some other dishonest excuse. We were dishonest with ourselves as well as with other people. We would never face ourselves as we really were or admit it when we were wrong. We pretended to ourselves that we were as good as the next fellow, although we suspected that we weren't. Before we met A.A. we were very *unloving*.

We usually neglect our families and are very unappreciative of our wives and children. Our few friends were only drinking companions, not real friends. Since we've been in A.A., we have made a start towards being more *unselfish*.

We no longer want our own way in everything. When things go wrong and we can't have what we want, we no longer sulk. We try not to waste money on ourselves. It makes us happy to see our families have enough money for themselves and the children. Since we've been in A.A. we have made a start towards becoming more *honest*.

We no longer have to lie to our family or our bosses. We try to be on time at our work and to earn what we get. We make an attempt to be honest with ourselves. We face ourselves as we really are. We have begun to find out what it means to be alive and to face the world honestly and without fear. Since we've been in A.A., we've made a start towards becoming more *loving* to our families and friends.

If our parents are alive, we show them our love again. We are more appreciative of our wives than we were, and we are truly grateful to them for putting up with us during our drinking. We find real companionship with our children. We feel that the friends we've found in A.A. are real friends. We begin to really care about other people, and our *resentments* leave us.

We stop pretending to be what we are not. We are content to be just ourselves. *The thoughts of an A.A. member on being yourself*:

"When I first came to A.A., I had considerable difficulty with the program, not in understanding it but in finding a way to apply it to my own self and my own life. Having arrived at A.A. in the usual condition, I found it difficult to think rationally and was forced to rely on the members of my group who were able to think clearly. This reliance, so necessary then, has become a part of my overall pattern of living.

In fact, I am certain that my so-called intelligence prior to A.A. only led me down the wrong paths. I am now happy to let the other fellow do my thinking for me. As a consequence, what I have of the A.A. program now is my own only insofar as I have accumulated and catalogued for my own use all the things I have heard and read in A.A. that appealed to me. In a sense, then, you could call me a sort of walking compendium of familiar quotations. I would like to pass along what many 'someones' have given to me and which I have found to be very helpful to me.

One obsessive fact of my alcoholism was the grandiose dreams. I can almost believe that I was used as a model from which the life of Walter Mitty was written. Getting sober did not relieve me of the habit-pattern of thinking that I was a much better person than was generally known. Thinking well of oneself seems to be a pretty common human trait. My obsession was that I believed what I was thinking. I had the 'genius' psychosis, I guess. Anyhow, it wasn't doing me any good. I could at least recognize that.

I came to believe that my salvation lay in the Fourth Step, the old 'know thyself' stuff. So I tore into Step Four like a hound dog at a coon. I can report that it had the calculated effect. I came out of that episode in a sorry state. When I read what I had put down on paper about myself, I was a most deflated specimen of humanity. When I say it had the calculated effect, I mean just the effect A.A. wanted.

I got humility. It hurt until I got accustomed to it, but it was what I needed.

Having taken a good look at myself and recovered from the shock, I went on to the next phase, attempting to repair the damage. Here is where I stumbled badly. I was attempting to rebuild this character into the person I thought I was. It didn't work. In my case at least, you can't make a silk purse out of a sow's ear. It took me a long time to discover this and I suffered somewhat, but again it had the desired effect. When the truth finally became apparent to me, I was ready to accept it.

Now that I know what I am, I am attempting to be what I am, instead of what I think I should be. Essentially, this has meant the lowering of my sights. Instead of sighting on the moon and bemoaning every shot wide of the mark, I now have my sights lowered to where I can sometimes score a hit on an earthly target. I can never run a four-minute mile or have Charlie's serenity or Mary's tolerance. I can only run as fast and have as much serenity and tolerance as befits me.

I find that being myself is every bit as hard as trying to be what I'm not, but that in the first instance I sometimes succeed, whereas in the last I always failed. When I failed, I suffered frustration and I can't stand very much of that.

Now I have learned to accept myself for what I am, not try to be what I'm not, I find that I'm catching up a little bit with Charlie on the serenity deal, as well as with some of the others in the things they have that I want. Funny part about it is that as soon as I stopped trying so hard, I started moving ahead. Sounds paradoxical doesn't it? All I know is that it works for me."

In taking our inventory, we try to be hard on ourselves and easy on others. We try to be constantly on the lookout for our own faults and defects of character and endeavor to correct them, at the same time being careful not to judge or condemn others. We should always be open to all good suggestions from others. *Above all, we should*:

Keep An Open Mind.

5. RESTITUTION

Easy Does It

The alcoholic is like a tornado roaring his way through the lives of others. Hearts are broken. Sweet relationships are dead. Affections have been uprooted. Selfish and inconsiderate habits have kept the home in a turmoil. Perhaps some people do come into A.A. with a fortunate record of having harmed only a few. We doubt, however, that anyone need turn in a blank piece of paper instead of a list of those they have harmed by their drinking; not if they think long enough and honestly enough. Even the rare quiet and so-called well-behaved alcoholic can make a list. And the ordinary variety of drunks, which the great majority of us are, can usually make a list from here to Timbuctoo, beginning with the spouse, the youngsters, the relatives, and the boss, and extending on through the people we borrowed from and didn't pay back, the people we lied to, and so on. The challenge of making amends is indeed a formidable matter to contemplate.

The Eighth Step in the A.A. program is: "Made a list of all persons we had harmed and became willing to make amends to them all." It was characteristic of many of us alcoholics to at least attempt to perform in a grandiose manner. And in harming others we usually succeeded magnificently. So to say that the Eighth Step is a large order, is to indulge in an understatement. And yet, however extended be the list of those we have harmed, the fulfillment of this step's admonition need not be a tedious or burdensome undertaking.

In the first place, let's examine the meaning of the verb "to amend." Webster's New International Dictionary defines it thus: "To make better, especially in character, to repair, restore, to free from faults, to put right, correct, rectify." There is a credo to which we of A.A. subscribe, the goal we hope to achieve through sobriety. The definition continues: "To change or modify in any way for the better; to recover from illness." This is what we are trying to do in Alcoholics Anonymous.

We feel that a person is unthinking when they say that sobriety is enough. He is like the farmer who came up out of his cyclone cellar to find his home ruined. To his wife he remarked: "Don't see anything the matter here, Ma. Ain't it grand the wind stopped blowin?" Yes, there is a long period of reconstruction ahead. We must take the lead.

A remorseful mumbling that we are sorry won't fill the bill at all. We ought to sit down with the family and frankly analyze the past as we now see it, being very careful not to criticize them. Our behavior will convince them more than our words. We must remember that ten or twenty years of drunkenness would make a skeptic out of anyone. Most of us had at least a few years of real pathological drinking behind us when we came into A.A. Those terrible years are the ones that become repulsive to us as we progress in our new-found life, years in which every action was influenced by alcoholic thinking, with all its implications. It naturally follows that whatever our state of life may be, those close to us bore the brunt of our outrageous behavior. How can one make amends to a dear wife or husband, daughter, son or parents, who through no fault of their own truly suffered physically, financially, and, more important, mentally, the humiliation and embarrassment of going through life with a drunkard?

A simple "I'm sorry, it won't happen again" is not enough. It is not enough for us and it is not enough for the aggrieved person. We have said it before: "I'm sorry." And sorry we stayed until the next bender. Then remorse set in and we couldn't stand it. And we became intoxicated again, because we felt so remorseful. Then we said: "I'm sorry" all over again. But that is not the way we say it this time, if we are sincere about making restitution.

What, for instance, of the business associates who took on some of our work during our absences from the office or on those days of the shakes and low efficiency? What of the friends whose time we wasted with such very boring blabber? And too, there are those intangible but damaging effects of the example we were to others; the good we might have done but didn't; the contributions we could have made to the helping of someone else in some way or just making a moment or two more pleasant, but didn't; the success of someone else we might have boosted along, but didn't. Anyone except a saint will find that they have harmed someone, somewhere, and that they have harmed society and their fellow men by failing to do the things for which they had the time, the talent, and the opportunity, but not the sense of *responsibility*.

The Ninth Step in our A.A. program is: "Made direct amends to such people whenever possible, except when to do so would injure them or others." This step is one calling for positive action. There is a world of difference between being willing to do a thing and actually doing it.

A sincere apology, with a true explanation to the person harmed of what we believe to be the reason for our past actions can quite frequently readjust personal relations, but the member of A.A. realizes that this cannot take care of the ones we have really hurt, and these are invariably the ones we love most.

Direct amends, by all means, is a must, in restoring physical property to the rightful owner, paying debts willingly within our ability to do so, and retracting the lie that hurt a reputation. But the real amends are made in being very careful of our day-to-day conduct and keeping "on the beam." The loved ones whom we have hurt don't want their "pound of flesh." Whether they are still in daily contact with us or not, amends are best made to them by restoring the love and confidence and respect they once had for us, by the *action* of right living.

Here in the Ninth Step is where we members of A.A. have a chance to prove ourselves, to redeem ourselves in the eyes of our loved ones; with our families first of all, with the ones we have made to suffer such keen anguish because of our uncontrolled drinking, to redeem ourselves in the sight of our friends and our business associates. Performing this step helps us to rid ourselves of the oppressing and tormenting feelings of remorse, of agitated memories and agonizing regrets. It helps us to regain a clear conscience, a peaceful, contented mind and some of our long-lost tranquility.

Amends are never to be made rashly or indiscriminately or without careful forethought. If we cause injury to others, it merely makes the existing lamentable situation more deplorable, and we are placing ourselves in a position where we will have to make amends for having tried to make amends. A general fiasco would result, of benefit to no one. There may be some wrongs which we can never fully make right. We don't worry about them, if we can honestly say to ourselves that we would right them if we could.

Some people cannot be seen. We send them an honest letter. And there may be a valid reason for postponement in some cases. But we don't delay if it can be avoided. We should be sensible, tactful, considerate and humble, without being servile or scraping. We don't crawl before anyone. If we are painstaking in our making of restitution, we will find a new freedom and happiness.

We're getting back again to acting like the sober people that we were once upon a time long ago and observing the little amenities of life, being courteous and considerate. Sometimes we can make indirect amends by admitting to ourselves and to God our past wrongs and humbly asking God's forgiveness in lieu of making direct amends. If the matter still presses heavily upon our conscience, we can if we wish talk the matter over with a person who has an understanding heart and a close mouth, one who will never violate our confidence.

In some instances even to make amends to some one person, such as a particularly hated enemy, seems more than anyone can undertake. But the willingness to swallow one's pride and take on even this difficult task is one of the most restorative experiences to be found. And the response we get is often unexpectedly good. An enemy has been transformed into a friend by our willingness to sincerely make what amends we can.

The point here is that in order to become willing to make amends, we have to admit to ourselves without reservations and without quibbling or reciting reasons why we inflicted the wrongs we did. We have to attain the attitude in which we say to ourselves that whether or not the other person was wrong or right, we at least were wrong to some extent, and we sincerely wish to right that wrong.

Reaching a degree of self-analysis and honesty which carries us to a willingness to make amends to all, helps to set the stage for the beginning of real progress in A.A., or real progress in any way of life. This restitution step is part of the conditioning process for attaining honesty, humility, and helpfulness; part of the process of fitting ourselves again into society, a very vital step in the rehabilitation of the alcoholic. The result of proper restitution is often a happy home life.

After we have made what amends we can, we start again with a clean slate. We begin to comprehend the word serenity and to know peace. No matter how far down the scale we have gone, we will begin to see how our experiences can benefit others. The feeling of uselessness and self-pity will disappear. We will become less selfish. Our attitude and outlook upon life will change. We will have more freedom and happiness. We will no longer "roar our way through the lives of others like a tornado." We will learn to walk more softly and with more consideration. *We will learn that* :

Easy Does It.

6. LIVE TODAY

Just For Today

In Alcoholics Anonymous, we learn to live one day at a time. All we have is today and if we don't take a drink today, we'll never take it, because it's always today. All we have is *now* and if we make the right use of the present moment, the past and the future will take care of themselves. Yesterday is gone, tomorrow never comes, today is here. *An old Sanskrit proverb says:*

"Look to this day. For it is life, the very life of life. In its brief course lie all the realities and verities of existence, the bliss of growth, the splendor of action, the glory of power. For yesterday is but a dream and tomorrow is only a vision. But today, well lived, makes every yesterday a dream of happiness and every tomorrow a vision of hope. Look well therefore to this day." Today is ours, to do with as we will. We have no other time.

Here is an item about yesterday, tomorrow and today, the author of which is unknown, but which is used extensively in A.A. literature:

"There are two days in every week about which we should not worry, two days which should be kept free from fear and apprehension. One of these days is yesterday, with its mistakes and cares, its faults and blunders, its aches and pains.

Yesterday has passed forever beyond our control. All the money in the world cannot bring back yesterday. We cannot undo a single act we performed, we cannot erase a single word we said. Yesterday is gone. The other day we should not worry about is tomorrow, with its possible adversities, its burdens, its large promise and poor performance.

Tomorrow is also beyond our immediate control. Tomorrow's sun will rise either in splendor or behind a mask of clouds, but it will rise. Until it does, we have no stake in tomorrow for it is as yet unborn. This leaves only one day--today. Any person can fight the battles of just one day. It is only when you and I add the burdens of those two awful eternities, yesterday and tomorrow, that we break down.

It is not the experience of today that drives people mad; it is remorse or bitterness for something which happened yesterday and the dread of what tomorrow may bring. Let us therefore live but one day at a time."

There is nothing new about the idea of living one day at a time. But it is a good idea for alcoholics, who seem to do a lot of worrying about the past and the future. *The author of the following is also unknown, and it carries out this same idea:*

"Life is given to us in allotments of one day at a time. The poorest has no less, the richest no more. Therefore, one day at a time should we live our lives and not try to take in more territory. Anybody can endure for twenty-four hours the burdens and griefs which would kill if continued over a lifetime.

On the same principle of day-by-day should we look to the improvement of mind, the development of body, the stiffening of will. Too often, vast plans for all these good resolutions fall to pieces because the individual has bitten off more than they can chew. Master one lesson well before passing on to the next. Build one good habit into the network of your responses before taking on others. See one good resolution through to the end.

At the same slow-but-sure pace, practice charity. The colossal needs of our day appall us, we have so little to give. But somewhere at hand there is a small need, well within our means. Give today to that. One good turn a day, the Boy Scouts call it. The sum total of these good deeds would make a ponderous book. Yet this book is being written on the basis of one day at a time. And, just for good measure, do each day at least one thing you'd prefer not to do. This has the effect of stretching moral muscles.

Take a hint from Mother Nature, who limits her children to one breath, one meal, one heartbeat, one step at a time. Don't crowd tomorrow. Don't drag yesterday behind you."

In A.A. we keep away from one drink for one day. You will never hear a member of A.A. make the statement: "I'll never take another drink as long as I live." We have said this too many times in the past and proved ourselves wrong by drinking again. We simply do not know what the future holds for us. We believe that the future is in the hands of our Higher Power. "The hand that veils the future is the hand of God."

When people come into A.A., they do not wish to contemplate the rest of their lives without a drink. It seems to them to be too much to undertake. So we advise them to do it one day at a time. People are so made that they can only carry the weight of twenty-four hours, no more. Directly they weigh themselves down with the years behind and the days ahead, their backs break. God has promised to help us with the burden of this day only. The Lord's Prayer puts it: "Give us this day our daily bread." If we are foolish enough to gather again the burden of the past and carry it, then indeed we cannot expect God to help us bear it.

So we advise the newcomer to A.A. to bite it off one day at a time. This makes the program much easier for them. "Life by the yard is hard; life by the inch is a cinch."

All we really have is *now*. We really have no past time and no future time. If we live right in the "now," the "nows" pile up behind us, stretching out into a long line. And this long line of past "nows" makes up a good past, if each "now" is properly lived. The future need not worry us, because when it becomes the "now," we will be able to handle it. We think of today as God's gift. Each morning, as we get out of bed, we thank God for giving us another day. We pray that we may do His will in it. We pray that we may be glad in it. We pray that we may perform some useful act today, perhaps help some other alcoholic. We pray that God will guide us today and help us to do the right thing.

The book, *Alcoholics Anonymous*, puts it this way: "On awakening, let us think about the twenty-four hours ahead. We consider our plans for the day. Before we begin, we ask God to direct our thinking. Our thought-lives will be placed on a much higher plane when we start the day with prayer and meditation. We conclude this period of meditation with a prayer that we will be shown through the day what our next step is to be. The basis of all our prayers is: Thy will be done in me and through me today."

Yesterday is gone. There is nothing we can do about it. It is "water under the bridge" or "water over the dam." We should not carry around a guilt complex. We are truly sorry for the evil things of our past, but there is nothing we can do about them after we have made what restitution we could. We can believe that God has forgiven us for all the things we did wrong in the past, providing that we are honestly trying to do the right thing today. It is better to try to forget the worst of our past, than it is to carry around a guilt complex with us today.

After we have made what restitution we could, we start each day with a clean slate. There is a saying that "opportunity knocks but once." This is not true. Every new day is a new opportunity to live as we should. The pages of the future are white as snow. We can write what we will on the page of each new day.

An alcoholic often uses their regret for the past and their apprehension of the future as an excuse to drink. *Here is how a member of A.A. feels about this:*

"Any alcoholic can give innumerable excuses for his past drinking. I always remember one of my pet alibis. A favorite tavern had a large sign behind the back bar which read: 'Free drinks tomorrow.' The sign remained permanently and I continued to come back daily, but tomorrow never came and of course no free drinks. So I kept on with my drinking, one day at a time.

By the same token, I can now stay sober only one day at a time. Right now--each instant as it passes--makes the past and the future. As I write or speak each word, it is only as of now. The next moment it is past, and there is no future except in my hopes for what I may say or do, if and when the time arrives.

In attending A.A. meetings and reading A.A. literature, I was constantly being reminded of the twenty-four hour program, the easy-does-it philosophy. Not until after a slip did the paralyzing thought come to me: 'Now is my future.'

To believe completely that the future is now, makes it possible for me to think ahead, look ahead, and work forward without worry about the consequences. Knowing that this moment--now--will always be my future gives me a new courage and satisfaction in living which I never fully enjoyed before. Instead of looking to the future as a distant heaven where I hoped and prayed that clutter and chaos would melt away and all my difficulties would solve themselves, I now believe that by diligent daily living, practical rules can be made to shape it, rules which evolve into principles for living each day as it comes. The courage born of making tomorrow part of today is described by Victoria Lincoln in her book, *The Art of Living*:

'Courage begins when we can admit that there is no life without some pain, some frustration; that there is no tragic accident to which we are immune; and that, beyond the normal exercise of prudence, we can do nothing about it. But courage goes on to see that the triumph of life is not in pains avoided but in joys completely lived, in the moment of their happening.

Courage lies in never taking so much as a good meal, a day of health, or fair weather for granted. It lies in learning to be aware of our moments of happiness as sharply as our moments of pain. We need not be afraid to weep when we have cause to weep, so long as we really rejoice at every cause for rejoicing.'

According to the ancient Chinese axiom, the longest journey begins with a single step. So also does our long journey of sobriety begin with a single day--the present moment--of sobriety. And it continues only so long as we stay sober for today--for this moment--now."

We should be happy today, because today is all we have. We should try to feel that "today is the best day of our lives." If we wait until some future time to be happy, if we postpone our happiness indefinitely, it may be too late when that time comes. God has broken up the years into night and day by the rising and setting of the sun. Each night is a small death, from which we may not awaken. Each new morning is a renewal of life.

Many of us in Alcoholics Anonymous feel that we are living on borrowed time. Many of our drinking companions are gone. We are very fortunate to be alive today. We in A.A. have the privilege of living two lives in one lifetime. One life of drunkenness, failure and defeat. Then, through the grace of God and A.A., another life of sobriety, happiness and usefulness. We have been given another chance to live. And we owe a debt of gratitude to A.A. that we can never repay as long as we live. As each new day dawns, we have a choice to make. We can take the path that leads to jail, insanity or death. Or we can take the path that leads to a reasonably happy and useful life. The choice is ours each day of our lives.

Our sobriety is a very serious thing to us. It is literally

a matter of life or death. What we do today may determine whether we live or die. *Here is the story of two alcoholics, one of whom found life in A.A., and the other who found death:*

"Chris did not know fear or love or friendship. Rugged, implacable, he gave no confidences. Light and laughter had been burned out of him. His eyes were like two chips of incandescent ice. Scars grooved his cheeks and eyebrows. His massive fists had battered many profiles into pulpy, reddened unconsciousness. He had finally killed a man. That was why he was caged in a police cell. 'A drunken swine' was what the doctor called him. Many others would have thought that this character reference was mild and had said worse, always when he was out of earshot.

One hundred and fifteen years ago, Chris' ancestors had pioneered this country, lumbered across its jagged mountains in cumbersome ox wagons. Many rivers had been forded, dyed red with the blood of their own dead. Waves of screaming savages had ripped gaping wounds into their wagon trains. There was no going back--return meant bondage, the horizon was freedom. Costly, yes, but free.

Chris too was on a quest for freedom. His enemy was invisibly fierce, a groping force within him that compelled him to seek relief from intolerable inner tension through alcohol, which gave to him the Aladdin's Lamp to drive all the demons temporarily away. They always came back to taunt and plague him, to goad him into further violence. The inferno in his brain crackled and roared, each drinking bout becoming more horrible. He was trapped with a terrifying vengeance.

A burly police sergeant opened the door of his cell.

'Why don't you stop drinking, man?' was his introductory sentence. Chris' eyes burned venomously but he made no sign he'd heard. He hated police particularly. Why does this big fool ask such a stupid question? Wouldn't he have stopped long ago, if only he knew how to? 'How?' was the sullen reply. 'We're letting you out on bail. I want you to promise me that for two days, forty-eight hours, you'll not take a drink. Today's Sunday and on Tuesday night I'll call for you and take you to a meeting of fellows who are known as Alcoholics Anonymous.' 'Ja. O.K., then. I'll be waiting for you Tuesday.'

That was how Chris found A.A. three years ago. The promise he made to the sergeant, he shifted to God. He also shrank it down from forty-eight hours to twenty-four hours. The murder charge was reduced to culpable homicide, as the edge of the curb had done the killing, not Chris' fists.

The drama of Chris' first meeting I shall always remember. I think back on it especially when my sense of value regarding my sobriety and emotional growth is sadly out of proportion, when troubles seem to snarl up the thread of gold that fuses us all together and the choking weed of self-pity flourishes in the topsoil of frustration. I can still see Chris in his blue suit, seated next to the sergeant. He sat waiting for the speaker to start. There was no smile on his lips, no geniality in his eyes, which burned like cold fire with a vast concentrated bitterness. He flashed them from face to face, listening, absorbing, watching. Occasionally he wiped his forehead and his hand was wet when it came away.

Finally he spoke: 'I want to join, if you want me.' Nothing more, not a wasted word. His cold suspicion had thawed. Chris' personality change, like water on granite, was slow but deadly sure. For some time he never spoke. Meeting after meeting he would take off his coat, tidy the room, clean the ash trays. When they used to heckle him in drunken, babbling tones, Chris was always the one who used to handle the 'difficult' boys.

His tolerance was unbelievable, his understanding of the sicker chaps was incredible. When he eventually spoke, the effect upon us was electrifying. His vivid descriptions of problems, situations and suggestions made weaker stomachs protest that his language would scare off the 'better class' of prospects. The majority felt that Chris' phraseology was like neat brandy, harsh in the beginning, but the afterglow was unbeatable. His sincerity and humility commanded admiration and respect.

Chris was a cabinetmaker--a good one. His boss knew that, and never yielded to the pressure to fire Chris. For this, Chris was grateful. The day arrived when he could repay this debt at a terrific cost to himself. Piet, the boss' son, was a hard and furious drinker. His derision at Chris' recovery and Chris' tolerance thereof could only be accomplished by a personality like Chris. Piet never missed an opportunity to insult or ridicule. Keeping a wary eye on Chris' fists, he rubbed salt into the wound with caustic remarks.

But the booze was catching up fast and Piet knew it. Ten months later, a worried father called Chris into his office and shutting the door to kill the noise of the workshop, he spoke: 'Piet's lying in bed, a drunken pig. I know he hates your guts. But would you go and knock some sense into him? He hasn't had food for two weeks. His wife's gone. I'm afraid he'll kill himself.' 'Now?' 'Right now--this morning. Don't worry about clocking out.'

An hour later Chris returned, very white, with tensed lips. Walking into the office, he said simply: 'Piet is not ready yet.' He didn't tell the father about the terrific strains that had been put upon his emotions at Piet's foul abuse. He never mentioned the wet blood on his left ear, where the brandy bottle had cut, in its flight from Piet's hand. That was all part of the game.

That afternoon, the boss hovered over Chris' bench. Despair was etched across his broad face. He was desperately awkward. 'Won't you try to help Piet again? I've just given him hell. I've told him that you're coming again. For me, Chris, will you go?' 'Ja, I'll try again.' Some time later the boss was walking through the workshop when, to his surprise, he saw Chris working away furiously at his bench. 'Why didn't you tell me you had come back?' he shouted, above the roar of the machinery. 'Is Piet cured?' 'Ja, Piet's cured all right,' shouted Chris. 'Good, then he'll never drink again.'

Chris came slowly towards the father, brushing the wood shavings out of his hair, until he was within an inch of the old man's face. 'Piet is cured of his drinking, Boss.' The words came slowly with great feeling. 'I found him in the kitchen with his head in the gas-filled oven.'"

What we do today may determine whether we live or die. We must make the right choices today. *Here is an article called "Just For Today" which is often used in A.A. literature, but whose author is not known:*

"*Just for today* I will try to live through this day only and not tackle my whole life problem at once. I can do something for twelve hours that would appall me if I felt that I had to keep it up for a lifetime.

Just for today I will be happy. This assumes to be true what Abraham Lincoln said, that 'most folks are as happy as they make up their minds to be.'

Just for today I will adjust myself to what is, and not try to adjust everything to my own desires. I will take my luck as it comes and fit myself to it.

Just for today I will try to strengthen my mind. I will study. I will learn something useful. I will not be a mental loafer. I will read something that requires effort, thought and concentration.

Just for today I will exercise my soul in three ways. I will do somebody a good turn, and not get found out. If anybody knows of it, it will not count. I will do at least two things I don't want to do, just for the exercise. I will not show anyone that my feelings are hurt. They may be hurt but today I will not show it.

Just for today I will be agreeable. I will look as well as I can, dress becomingly, act courteously, criticize not one bit, not find fault with anything, and try not to improve or regulate anybody except myself.

Just for today I will have a program. I may not follow it exactly, but I will have it. I will save myself from two pests, hurry and indecision.

Just for today I will be unafraid. Especially I will not be afraid to enjoy what is beautiful and to believe that, as I give to the world, so the world will give to me."

If we are following the A.A. program, we will try to forget the past and not worry about the future, because we are made to carry the load of today only. *For contented recovery, we learn to live:*

Just for Today.

7. SERVICE

Am I My Brother's Keeper?

The way of Alcoholics Anonymous is the way of service. Without that, it would not work. We have been "on the wagon" and hated it. We have taken the pledge and waited with impatience for the time to be up, so we could drink again. We have tried in all manner of ways to help ourselves. But not until we begin to try to help other alcoholics do we get full relief.

It is an axiom that the A.A. program has to be given away in order to be kept. We get and then we give. If we do not give, we do not keep. We have found that service to others makes the world a good place. In fact, civilization would cease if each person was always out only for himself.

We alcoholics have a wonderful opportunity to contribute to the well-being of the world. We have a common problem and we have found a common answer. What a wonderful world it would be if everybody took their own greatest problem and, having found the answer to it, spent the rest of their lives helping others with the same problem! Soon we would have the right kind of a world.

The essence of A.A. is one alcoholic who is sober talking to an alcoholic who is still drinking, telling them their own experience with drinking, how they recovered through the A.A. program and so helping the other person to see the light. Each recovered A.A. is a modern miracle. *Here is the story of such a miracle:*

"There was a movie called 'Miracle on 34th Street' in

which some wondrous things took place. It was a Hollywood version of a 'spiritual experience' in which not only the individual characters but even Macy's and Gimbel's saw the simple wisdom of 'live and let live.' In a great burst of brotherhood, Macy's recommended Gimbel's and Gimbel's sent customers to Macy's. This was a mercantile miracle. And it was profitable for all--Macy's, Gimbel's, and even the customers.

Just the other night, we heard of another 'Miracle on 34th Street.' This was an A.A. miracle. It took place late at night. West 34th Street was practically deserted. There were no grinding cameras, no klieg lights, no director telling the actors what to do. The cast of characters consisted of two men, both drunks. They knew each other by sight, having met previously in darkened doorways or in some broken-down gin mill in New York's west side. One drunk had that day collected his relief check and was pretty well along with his drinking.

As he staggered along 34th Street, a pint of fairly drinkable whiskey in his pocket, he spied a familiar face. He couldn't remember the name, nor even where he'd seen the guy before. But he did know that here was a kindred spirit. Hallelujah! 'Have a drink, pal! Have a li'l drink.' 'No!' 'Whaddya mean, no? Whassa matter? Look, this ish good stuff!' Whereupon, the first drunk, to prove he was a reliable host and no Borgia, tilted the bottle and took a good belt. 'Aaaah!' he sighed and offered the flask to his companion again. 'Come on, have a li'l drink, pal!'

'No!' said the other man firmly, 'I've just come from a meeting of Alcoholics Anonymous. I've just found out that maybe I won't ever have to drink again. I'm on my way to get a bus and go home!'

The man with the bottle just stood there, trying to get such a crazy statement through his beclouded mind. He took another swig and shuffled on down the street. Then he stopped, turned and retraced his steps -- to the bus station. He was in time to find his pal inside a bus, waiting for it to pull out. Without ceremony, he stuck his head inside and said: 'Hey -- write that thing down for me. Maybe that's for me too!'

Next day a disheveled 'bum' turned up at the A.A. Intergroup Office, clutching a grimy bit of paper with the address of A.A. on it. Today, that man has been sober 16 months, a fine A.A. and a fine man. That is A.A.'s miracle on 34th Street. It won no Academy Award. Maybe because it isn't fantasy but fact. To A.A. it is almost routine, a miracle we've seen a thousand times.

There is an old saying that truth is stranger than fiction. We of A.A. know from our own experiences that 'coincidences' which happen so often are not coincidences at all. We know that a Higher Power daily and hourly on 34th Street and any other street performs miracles which even Hollywood would call fantasy."

One of the finest things about A.A. is the sharing. Sharing is a wonderful thing because the more you share the more you have. In our old drinking days we didn't do much sharing. We used to keep things to ourselves, partly because we were ashamed, but mostly because we were selfish. And we were very lonely because we didn't share. When we came into A.A., the first thing we found was sharing. We heard other alcoholics frankly sharing their experiences with hospitals, jails, and all the usual mess that goes with drinking.

What impresses us most at an A.A. meeting is the willingness to share, without holding anything back. And pretty soon we find ourselves sharing also. We start telling our own experiences and by so doing we help the other person. And when we've got these things off our chest, we feel a lot better. It does us a lot of good to share with some other poor unfortunate person who's in the same box that we were in. And the more we share with them, the more we have left for ourselves. *Here is the story of the coat that belongs to A.A.:*

"This is the story of a coat; just the story of a friendly garment, an A.A. garment. It was back in about 1943. A small group of the lads were congregated in Henry's barber shop, talking of this and that. Henry, let it be known, is a grade A, practicing A.A. Somehow, the conversation got around to the raggedness of some of the new boys, fresh from the gutter, their last decent piece of clothing probably hocked for a crock of high-voltage wine. 'It's hard for them to get jobs. It's tough to have to attend meetings in rags.' 'It's rugged to try to get your self-respect back when the stuff you're wearing is patched and threadbare.' And so on, into the afternoon.

But out of that gabfest came a practical idea. We would assemble a 'rag-bag.' Cast-off suits, shoes, shirts, underwear, socks, neckties, or what have you in the way of cast-offs, but still presentable. Henry volunteered to keep the stuff in his barber shop and see that it was kept clean.

The idea was that down-and-outers could 'borrow' outfits and then return them after they had got on their feet, and could buy clothes of their own.

At just about that time, the well-to-do father of one of our members died, leaving behind him a virtually brand new overcoat that had cost in the neighborhood of $150. It was far too small for the son, so he pitched it into the rag-bag. That was in 1943. A few days ago, I was in Henry's barbershop when a chap I had known as a drunk and down-and-outer walked in. I looked at him a couple of times. 'Say, Henry,' I asked, 'isn't that the overcoat?' 'Yep,' grinned Henry, 'That's the coat. He's the twenty-first to wear it.' 'And it came back all those times?' 'Well, yes, in a manner of speaking.' And he gave me the highlights.

'You remember Jasper M.?' Henry asked. I remembered that Jasper had given A.A. a brief whirl and then died in a hospital of pneumonia. That is, they called it pneumonia that killed him, but a lot of us knew better. 'Well, Jasper was wearing that coat when the cops picked him up out of a snowbank. The coat was soaked and so was he. After he died, I got it back from the hospital.'

Then there was another time. One of the boys dropped into the barbershop. 'Say, Henry,' he said, 'I think I just saw that prize overcoat of yours in the gutter down on Blank Street.' 'Good Lord, man,' Henry was genuinely disturbed, 'why didn't you bring it in?' 'Oh, it's all muddy and I didn't think you wanted it.' But Henry didn't hear him. He grabbed his hat and was heading for Blank Street on the gallop. Tenderly he picked up the muddy garment and took it to a cleaner.

'One guy brought it back, not because he had so-bered up but because Spring and warm weather had come,' Henry mused, 'and I've pulled it out of hock shops.' But there's the bright side. Out of the twenty-one who had worn the coat, fifteen had succeeded in A.A., had found jobs, bought new clothes, and returned the old coat for the next fellow.

And that, my friends, is a pretty fair average. I suspect that the old coat has had a lot to do with the sobriety of quite a few men. Henry has guarded that now well-worn garment, just as he would guard an A.A. 'baby.'"

The Twelfth Step in the A.A. program is as follows: "Having had a spiritual awakening as the result of these steps, we tried to carry the message to alcoholics and to practice these principles in all our affairs." The first thing is to become spiritually awakened by studying and following the A.A. program. You cannot give away what you haven't got. So we have to make the program part of ourselves in order to be effective in helping others.

The *first* thing in trying to help another alcoholic is to get their confidence. We do this by telling them our own experiences with drinking, so that they see that we know what we are talking about. If we share our experiences frankly, they will know that we are sincerely trying to help them. They will realize that they are not alone in their illness and that others have had experiences as bad or worse than theirs. This gives them confidence that they can be helped.

The *second* thing is to encourage their confidences and their confession of their own experiences. By frankly sharing with the prospect, we get them talking about their own experiences. They will open up and confess things to us that they haven't been able to tell other people. And they feel better when this confession has got these things off their chest. It's a great load off their mind to get these things out into the open. It's the things that are kept hidden that fester in the heart and weigh on the mind. They feel a sense of release and freedom after they have opened up their hearts to us.

The *third* thing is to convince the prospect and encourage this conviction. The prospect must be convinced that their lives have become unmanageable and are seriously disturbed by their drinking. They must face the fact that they must do something constructive about their drinking. They must try to be honest with themselves and try to face themselves as they really are. They must be convinced that they must do something about their drinking and they must be made to see that their whole life may depend upon this conviction.

The *fourth* thing is to bring about a change in the prospect, so that they experience a form of conversion. *Conversion means change.* The prospect must learn to change their way of thinking. Until now, almost everything they have done has been connected in some way with drinking. Now they must face a new kind of a life -- without liquor. They must be made to feel that they can't overcome their drinking by their own will power -- that they can't fight liquor -- so they must turn to a power greater than themselves for the strength they need. This conversion to a belief in a Higher Power comes gradually, as they try it and find that it works.

The *fifth* thing is to continue with the prospect as long as is necessary. Continuance means our staying with them until they have a foothold in this new way of living. We should stay with them and encourage them to attend meetings regularly. They will soon learn that following the program is a lot easier in fellowship with others who are trying to do the same things. We should continue to help them by keeping in touch with them, so that they don't get out of touch with A.A. Continuance is another name for good sponsorship.

Another form of Twelfth Step work is starting new A.A. groups. *Here is the story of one who found that it was not so much her own efforts as the grace of God who inspired her in this work:*

"When I was twenty-two months in A.A., I landed in Dallas, Texas, a lone female carrying the A.A. torch in one hand and the A.A. book in the other. I was weighed down by a terrific feeling of responsibility -- I had to start a group, I *had* to do it. I felt very inadequate. I wanted to 'build a home in a day.' I met with lots of opposition. I met with disappointments until I woke up and found the key to the situation. Too much 'I,' too much self in the whole deal. 'I' had only one responsibility, that of keeping 'I' sober. What did that entail? Daily contact with A.A., a daily bit of positive A.A. work, daily true and thoughtful gratitude. Leave the results in the hands of this 'Power greater than I.' And from then on, the results have amazed me.

For those who would like to know what my 'daily bits' were, I'll list a few. Seeing doctors, ministers, the Y.M.C.A.,

Salvation Army, talking A.A. to anyone who would listen. I rented a post-office box and sent the number of the box to our national secretary, so that inquiries for help could come through that source. Soon the days became weeks, weeks became months -- and there was a group. When the group was five months old, a plea came for me to help get something going in San Antonio.

Down I went with two of the Dallas 'babies.' For three days and nights we did our A.A. bit with burning zeal. We did all we could and left feeling very hopeful, but nothing 'caught fire.' In a few weeks, we thought our trip had been in vain. That old 'I' trouble reared its ugly head. Maybe if I could have stayed on the spot, doing all the things there that I had done here, maybe I could have made it go.

A year and a half later, another plea came from San Antonio. So down I went with the same burning zeal, but worked no harder than before, and in one week rounded up four 'alkies,' three females and one male. The male was a man we'd contacted on the previous trip. This time, he happened to be ready to grab the torch out of my hand and so everything 'caught on fire.'

In just a year, San Antonio had a vital and growing group. I visited them a month later and stayed ten days. But all they've done since has been through their own efforts, not mine. 'I' definitely wasn't needed on the spot. The complete death, I hope, of the 'I' trouble has come through my experience with a group in the U.S. Disciplinary Barracks at North Camp Hood, Texas.

I've sponsored it solely through correspondence for a year and a half. The rule 'No females allowed' kept me away from the Barracks, but every week I've written to the two men who contacted me. They kept doggedly on till they had a group. Now the group, through its own efforts, with no help from the outside, has gained all the respect and notice that it deserves. Eventually a letter from none other than the Commander of the Camp arrived, inviting this female to visit the group.

At the beginning of this article, I said I'd found the key, that the results always lie in the hands of a Power greater than I -- and it is the one that fits. This key is not mine, so I can't feel in any way responsible. To me, the groups are as miraculous as my own sobriety. They are God's doing and both awe me in a wondrous way."

In the story of the Good Samaritan, the wayfarer fell among robbers and was left lying in the gutter, half dead, and a priest and a Levite passed by on the other side of the road. But the Good Samaritan was moved with compassion and came to him and bound up his wounds and brought him to an inn and took care of him. A lot of well meaning people treat an alcoholic like the priest and the Levite. They pass by on the other side by scorning them and telling them what low people they are, with no will power. Whereas, they really have fallen for alcohol in the same way that the man in the story fell among robbers. And the member of A.A. who is working with other alcoholics is like the Good Samaritan. They are moved with compassion. They go to another alcoholic and bind up their wounds of the spirit and take them to an inn or an A.A. meeting, and take care of them until they can care for themselves.

In Alcoholics Anonymous we learn that since we are

alcoholics we can be uniquely useful people. That is, we can help another alcoholic, when somebody who has not had our experience with drinking could not help them. This fact makes us uniquely useful. The members of A.A. are a unique group of people because they have taken their own greatest defeat and failure and sickness, and used it as a means of helping others. We who have been through the mill are the ones who can best help other alcoholics. We who have learned to put our drink problem in God's hands can help others to do so. We can be used as a connection between an alcoholic's need and God's supply of strength. We in A.A. can be uniquely useful, because we have the misfortune (or fortune) to be alcoholics ourselves.

The last part of the Twelfth Step says: "and to practice these principles in all our affairs." This means carrying the A.A. program into our everyday life -- at home, in the office, at work, and among people everywhere. The Twelve Steps of the program are guide posts. They point the way for us to go. They put before us goals that we will never fully reach, but the striving for these goals makes for a happy and contented way of life. By following them, we have a life purpose which really makes life worth living. *Here is a Magna Carta for members of A.A.:*

"I recognize the fact that I shall always be an alcoholic and that I can therefore live a contented normal life only as long as I completely refrain from drinking alcohol. I believe that I am wholly honest in my desire not to drink. However, I realize that after a long period of sobriety, I might be deceived into believing that I could again become a moderate drinker.

To safeguard myself against this danger, I promise myself that before taking the first drink, I will get in touch with another alcoholic in whose judgment I have confidence. Knowing of no sound reason why I should ever drink again, I am prepared to wage relentless war on all my resentments against others and to attack intolerance in myself tirelessly, as well as to modify the resentments and intolerance of others with whom I come in contact, wherever I gracefully can.

Whenever I find myself unable to discover the reason for intolerance or resentment in myself, I will gladly seek the assistance of a friend or counselor in discovering and uprooting them at the source. Self-honesty is necessary to self-respect and neither of them can be spared in gaining the respect and trust of others. Therefore, I am committed to examining my actions critically and questioning my motives for my way of behavior at least once daily, being always sure to delay action or judgment when I am unsure of the proper course.

Knowing that when I am tense, prejudice tends to take the place of judgment, sensitivity of self-esteem, and selfishness of consideration for others, I recognize my need to practice relaxation with regularity, not least because it is one of the best safeguards for sobriety. Whenever I may be commended for my will power in overcoming alcoholism, I will carefully explain that alcoholism is an incurable illness which can only be arrested by one's achieving emotional maturity, and that every effort to effect a 'cure' through will power sooner or later is certain to prove itself a failure.

I recognize that the Golden Rule can be practically

applied, and I accept it as a guide to lead me away from self-satisfaction and over-confidence, and towards continuous improvement of my personal relations with others, as well as towards discharging my social responsibilities in general. If I can wisely and competently counsel anyone who sincerely requests my aid, I shall endeavor to do so willingly. However, in such instances I shall attempt to remember that since everyone has the right to solve their own problems, I must not force them to accept my views.

It will therefore be my aim to give what aid I can, in guiding them toward the discovery of themselves. Realizing that to face reality, one must maintain an open mind, I shall endeavor to be receptive always to a new idea and constantly let new insights have a normal growth within me.

Realizing the close kinship that exists between idle dreaming and excessive drinking, I shall endeavor to keep my dreams trained on practical objectives which are attainable and force them thus to serve as aids to my ideas and plans. As far as I am able, I will endeavor to make my aims unselfish, keeping them directed towards the common good, without reference to my personal needs, and thereby shall regard my own requirements to be satisfied by my earned and increasing share in the common weal." *Here is a "Credo" for an A.A. member:*

"I am glad to be a part of Alcoholics Anonymous, of that great fellowship which is spreading all over the world. I am only one of many A.A.s, but I am one. I am grateful to be living at this time, when I can help A.A. to grow, when it needs me to put my shoulder to the wheel and help keep the message going.

I am glad to be able to be useful, to have a reason for living, to have a purpose in life. I want to lose my life in this fellowship and so find it again. I need the A.A. principles for the development of the buried life within me, that good life which I had misplaced but which I found again in this fellowship. This life within me is developing slowly but surely, with setbacks and mistakes, but still developing. I cannot yet know what it will be, but I know that it will be good. That's all I want to know, it will be good.

A.A. may be human in its organization, but it is divine in its purpose. The purpose is to point me toward the God of my understanding and the good life. My feet have been set upon the right path. I feel it in the depths of my being. I am going in the right direction. The future can be safely left to my Higher Power. Whatever the future holds, it cannot be too much for me to bear. I have the Divine Power with me, to carry me through everything that may happen.

Participating in the privileges of the A.A. fellowship, I shall share in the responsibilities, taking it upon myself to carry my fair share of the load, not grudgingly but joyfully. I am deeply grateful for the privileges I enjoy because of my membership in the A.A. way of life. They put an obligation upon me which I will not shirk. I will gladly carry my fair share of the burdens. Because of the joy of doing them, they will no longer be burdens but opportunities.

I shall not wait to be drafted for service to my fellow travelers, but I shall volunteer. I shall accept every opportunity to work for A.A. as a challenge and I shall do my best to accept every challenge and perform my task as best I can.

I shall be loyal in my attendance, generous in my giving, kind in my criticism, creative in my suggestions, loving in my attitudes. I shall give A.A. my interest, my enthusiasm, my devotion, and most of all, myself."

We in Alcoholics Anonymous know the joy of giving. We believe that when we come to the end of our lives, it will be only the things that we have given away that we will take with us. We will take no material thing with us, but we will take with us the kind words we have said, the kind deeds we have done, the help we may have given to our fellow alcoholics.

We alcoholics, who have been helped to find A.A. by someone who was interested in our welfare, believe that we are under a deep obligation to pass the message on to others. We members of Alcoholics Anonymous believe in this with all our hearts: *If an alcoholic needs help and asks for help:*

I Am My Brother's Keeper.

THE TWELVE STEPS OF A.A.

1.   We admitted we were powerless over alcohol -- that our lives had become unmanageable.

2.   Came to believe that a Power greater than ourselves could restore us to sanity.

3.   Made a decision to turn our will and our lives over to the care of God *as we understood Him.*

4.   Made a searching and fearless moral inventory of ourselves.

5.   Admitted to God, to ourselves, and to another human being the exact nature of our wrongs.

6.   Were entirely ready to have God remove all these defects of character.

7.   Humbly asked Him to remove our shortcomings.

8.   Made a list of all persons we had harmed, and became willing to make amends to them all.

9.   Made direct amends to such people wherever possible, except when to do so would injure them or others.

10.   Continued to take personal inventory and when we

were wrong promptly admitted it.

11.   Sought through prayer and meditation to improve
        our conscious contact with God *as we understood
        Him,* praying only for knowledge of His will for us
        and the power to carry that out.

12.   Having had a spiritual awakening as the result of
        these steps, we tried to carry this message to alcohol-
        ics, and to practice these principles in all our affairs.

THE TWELVE TRADITIONS OF A.A.

1.   Our common welfare should come first; personal
        recovery depends upon A.A. unity.

2.   For our group purpose there is but one ultimate
        authority -- a loving God as He may express Himself
        in our group conscience. Our leaders are but trusted
        servants; they do not govern.

3.   The only requirement for A.A. membership is a
        desire to stop drinking.

4.   Each group should be autonomous except in matters
        affecting other groups or A.A. as a whole.

5.   Each group has but one primary purpose -- to carry
        its message to the alcoholic who still suffers.

6.   An A.A. group ought never endorse, finance or lend the A.A. name to any related facility or outside enterprise, lest problems of money, property and prestige divert us from our primary purpose.

7.   Every A.A. group ought to be fully self-supporting, declining outside contributions.

8.   Alcoholics Anonymous should remain forever non-professional, but our service centers may employ special workers.

9.   A.A., as such, ought never be organized, but we may create service boards or committees directly responsible to those they serve.

10.   Alcoholics Anonymous has no opinion on outside issues; hence the A.A. name ought never be drawn into public controversy.

11.   Our public relations policy is based on attraction rather than promotion; we need always maintain personal anonymity at the level of press, radio and films.

12.   Anonymity is the spiritual foundation of all our Traditions, ever reminding us to place principles before personalities.

Other titles by Richmond Walker:

For Drunks Only: One Man's Reaction to Alcoholics Anonymous
40 pp.

Twenty-Four Hours a Day
384 pp.

Available from:

Hazelden Educational Materials
Pleasant Valley Road
Box 176
Center City, MN 55012-0176
(612) 257-4010
(800) 328-9000

Other titles available from Glen Abbey Books
PO Box 19762, Seattle, WA. 98109
Order Toll Free: 1-800-782-2239

_____ 14-7	Evening Prayers Morning Promises	$7.95
_____ 15-5	Stepping Stones to Recovery: for Women	$6.95
_____ 16-3	The 7 Points of Alcoholics Anonymous	$6.95
_____ 08-2	AA The Way It Began	$8.95
_____ 06-6	Coming Home	$7.95
_____ 05-8	A Year to Remember	$9.95
_____ 04-X	Stepping Stones to Recovery	$8.95
_____ 01-5	A Reference Guide to the Big Book of AA	$9.95

I understand that I may return any book for a full refund if not satisfied.

Visa/MC: # _____ Exp: _____

Name: _____

Address: _____

_____ Zip: _____

Wash. State Residents add 8.1% tax.

Shipping: $2.00 for the first book and 50c for each additional book.

Glen Abbey Books 1-800-782-2239